Winnetka-Northfield Public Library

3 1240 00542 8797

OCT -- 2015

LIBERATION

WITHDRAWN

D1377763

WINNETKA-NORTHFIELD
PUBLIC LIBRARY DISTR.
WINNETKA, IL 60093
847-446-7220

LIB ERA TION

New Works on Freedom from Internationally Renowned Poets

Foreword by HA JIN

Edited and Introduced by MARK LUDWIG

Beacon Press, Boston

Beacon Press
Boston, Massachusetts
www.beacon.org

Beacon Press books
are published under the auspices of
the Unitarian Universalist Association of Congregations.

© 2015 by Mark Ludwig, Terezín Music Foundation
All rights reserved

All of the poems in *Liberation* are published here for the first time, except the following, which appear in *Liberation* with permission of the poets and their publishers:

"Moksha," by Meena Alexander, is reprinted by permission of the publisher of *Atmospheric Embroidery* (New Delhi: Hachette India, 2015).

"Trayvon-Redux," by Rita Dove, appeared in *Killing Trayvons: An Anthology of American Violence*, edited by Kevin Alexander Gray, JoAnn Wypijewski, and Jeffrey St. Clair (Counterpunch, 2014).

The landays by Afghani women appeared in *I Am a Beggar of the World: Landays from Contemporary Afghanistan*, translated and edited by Eliza Griswold (Farrar, Straus and Giroux, 2014).

"No Casualties Reported," by Agi Mishol, appeared in *Ha'aretz*. Translated by Joana Chen.

"Samurai Song," by Robert Pinsky, appeared in *Jersey Rain*. © Farrar, Straus and Giroux.

"Poem of Disconnected Parts," by Robert Pinsky, appeared in *Gulf Music*. © 2007 by Robert Pinsky. Reprinted by permission of Farrar, Straus and Giroux.

"The Foundation," by C. K. Williams, appeared in *Wait* (Farrar, Straus and Giroux).

Printed in the United States of America
18 17 16 15   8 7 6 5 4 3 2 1

This book is printed on acid-free paper that meets the uncoated paper
ANSI/NISO specifications for permanence as revised in 1992.

Text design and composition by Wilsted & Taylor Publishing Services

Library of Congress Cataloging-in-Publication Data
Liberation : new works on freedom from internationally renowned poets / edited and
introduced by Mark Ludwig ; foreword by Ha Jin.
     pages cm
   ISBN 978-0-8070-0027-4 (paperback)—ISBN 978-0-8070-4188-8 (hardcover)—
   ISBN 978-0-8070-4190-1 (ebook)
1. Liberty—Poetry. 2. World War, 1939–1945—Concentration camps—
Liberation—Poetry. 3. World War, 1939–1945—Poetry. I. Ludwig, Mark, editor.
II. Jin, Ha, 1956– writer of foreword. III. Title: New works on freedom from
internationally renowned poets.
   PN6110.L43L53 2015
   808.81'93581—dc23   2015015260

Contents

PART I
"so they might know what liberation is"

PART IV
"a ghost of gunmetal drones overhead"

PART V
"Death sails into the gilded ballroom in purple satin"

PART VI

"Speak when broken"

PART VII
"think of the trapped wren"

A MATTER OF SPIRIT

This engaging volume has gathered recent poems by more than sixty poets across the world. Many of the poems were translated from other languages, and together they represent a spirit that confronts what has damaged and still endangers human existence. Some of the poems are rooted in historical happenings, to which the poets give nuances and their own perspectives. Some are based on human drama, mostly metaphorical, without specific temporal reference. Yet one way or another, they all shed light on the theme of liberation.

On the other hand, the theme of liberation creates new interpretive possibilities for these poems. As I was reading, I kept wondering how the poems could be read in such a light. How can a poem about Whitney Houston be associated with the idea of liberation? At first glance, the connection seems tenuous. However, I soon realized that poet Kwame Dawes's perception of Houston's life and death showed a lot of relevance and acute insight—even though she was a celebrity, her freedom was conditioned and limited, shaped by numerous social forces hostile to liberation. A poem like Han Dong's "Story" is about a couple parting ways. By nature, such a poem is metaphorical and atemporal, but if we think about it from the perspective of liberation, we can see that the couple's separation, temporary or permanent, is indeed a kind of liberation. But who is liberated? Maybe the one who stays? Maybe the one who leaves? Or maybe both? Interpretive opportunities like those can be mind-opening and delightful.

One feature shared by these poems is a serious engagement with the world. In this regard, the poems demonstrate a willingness to oppose what has debased and violated humanity. Conventionally, poetry is supposed to remember so as to preserve, and in a conservative sense, it is also supposed to reconcile conflicts and inspire confidence. Many of these poems, however, break those norms and seem to perform more urgent functions. They remind us of injustice and warn us against the violence that continues to spread.

Robert Pinsky's lines in "Poem of Disconnected Parts" refer to the cycle of deadly forces embodied in a few women's lives:

> Becky is abandoned in 1902 and Rose dies giving
> Birth in 1924 and Sylvia falls in 1951.
>
> Still falling still dying still abandoned in 2005
> Still nothing finished among the descendants.

Indeed, facing such perpetual "falling" and "dying," poetry must first make people aware of them. It's essential for a poet to stand aside from the collective and speak in a dissonant voice that reminds people of reason and human cost and to warn them against the destructive hands that operate overtly, often under the aegis of grandiloquent rhetoric. I would say that the strength of these poems lies in the fact that they do not avoid being useful or serving a purpose. In truth, poetry ought to be more useful nowadays, so as to become more relevant in our diminishing reading culture.

While sounding strident, some of these poems still give a lot of pleasure and celebrate our existence. They remind us of the joy of being alive and able to work and do something decent. They compel us to appreciate the possibilities of life while commiserating with those who are deprived of them. They are moving partly because they show that we still can dream and sing. These lines from Anita Endrezze's poem "There Is No Cure for MS" exemplify an imagined happiness:

> If there was a way to liberate my body
> from disease, I'd dance across lily pads,
> balanced between sky and water.

If I knew the abracadabra that cures,
I'd follow the sun across mountains,
laughing at the magic of walking.
I'd quicken my veins with lightning.
If if if I could be healed,
I'd sing of the shining paths
hummingbirds trace
in the fragrant air   O Joy!
and strum the spell-bound moon
with my slender fingers.

Lines like those display an indomitable spirit in confronting the adversary forces that diminish humanity. That is a kind of triumph.

HA JIN

Introduction

LIBERATION

On May 8, 1945, the Terezín (Theresienstadt) concentration camp was the last of the more than 42,500 Nazi camps and ghettos to be liberated. Among this network of mass annihilation there were extermination centers, concentration camps, forced labor camps, Jewish ghettos, POW camps, and T-4 "euthanasia" sites. Between 1933 and 1945, fifteen to twenty million people died or were imprisoned in this constellation of unfathomable horrors, brutality, and deprivation.* The victims included much of European Jewry, as well as political dissidents, homosexuals, Sinti and Roma, and POWs.

Their liberation seventy years ago was the inspiration behind this initiative to create a Liberation Project for poetry and music on a global scale. Over the course of the last two years, I have reached out to poets around the world to invite them to participate. Their only instruction was to create a new work based on the theme of liberation, what it meant to them and how it resonated and manifested in their own life experience. I have been deeply humbled not only by the overwhelming response from this group of artists, but also by the gift of interacting with each and every one of them.

This anthology includes more than sixty poets from twenty-seven countries offering a worldview of what liberation means to some of the great voices and minds of our age. The collection is also meant to illustrate the human yearning for freedom and the right to determine our own destinies. This is so beautifully exemplified in Dunya Mikhail's poem "Ama-ar-gi." *Ama-ar-gi* is a Sumerian

* Statistics provided by Geoffrey P. Megargee, editor of *The United States Holocaust Memorial Museum Encyclopedia of Camps and Ghettos, 1933–1945* (Bloomington: Indiana University Press, 2009).

cuneiform glyph believed to be the first known word for freedom. The poet is contemporary, the language ancient; however, the concept and desire for freedom is a timeless and human aspiration.

> *Thus, like all of you*
> *we breathe Ama-ar-gi*
> *and before we shed our first tears*
> *we weep Ama-ar-gi*

Poets have a unique gift of encouraging us to alter the lens of our day-to-day perspective. Like a kaleidoscope with its mirrors reflecting ever-changing patterns, many of these poems are filled with a rich language of images and perspectives that surprise, move, and challenge us.

This anthology is divided into eight sections, each headed by a quote from among this collection of poems that epitomizes a particular aspect of liberation. Many of these poems could belong in multiple categories—a further testament to their depth, resonance, and range. They travel freely in realms of remembrance, healing, and transformation. Individually and collectively, they offer us a space for inspiration, introspection, and hope. It is with great anticipation and excitement for the journey upon which you the reader are about to embark that I introduce you to this beautiful anthology.

MARK LUDWIG

PART I

"so they might know what liberation is"

On Being Asked to Write a Poem on the Theme of Liberation

RICHARD HOFFMAN

I wish I understood what liberation is;
but history seems to come down to this:
behind us cut sod and a mound of soil,

a trench of jerky and bone, each skull
stained and broken, an empty husk.
Our truck gasps and grinds as dusk

shifts day's hoarse gears a second time,
a dismal sound that will forever rhyme
with respite but never catharsis.

I wish I understood what liberation is.
I looked for something I could quote,
but Ecclesiastes reads like a suicide note,

and cheap grace, as the martyred Pastor
Bonhoeffer called it, that instant Easter
resurrecting victims and perps alike,

is our most cowardly mistake:
after such knowledge, what? What?
Don't. Don't speak the word. To liberate

our children's children's children,
maybe, provide them with an antigen
of an idea, maybe we can manage that

if we begin right now to search for it,
forsaking safety, comfort, solace,
so they might know what liberation is.

After Liberation

JULIE CARR

After the philosophers gathered in the park under heavy sky. After the children ran to the trees waving sticks and then hid. After teens sulked. After flags. After the city changed. After erotic grass tips. After standing on our hands. Beautiful cloudy girl bikes by. Aged man with camera shoots the grill. We depart from all that is reasonable. After the lips rubbing. After the gravestones and the unmarked graves. After they forced the women to walk among the exhumed bodies of the dead. After she walked among the bodies of the children beginning to rot. After her own children became noxious to her. After the confrontation in which he realized she meant to place him inside her enormous purse and close the clasp. Ships, timber icy, waiting in the bay. After sunrise the sailors approached the shore. Slept on sand with bellies exposed, wounds oozing rivulets of blood. After blood. After the German health worker devoured her steak. After six weeks in Mexico City and six further weeks in Colombia. After the dictators. The smoker sulked. The boy played war until the girl came and then they ran. Flowers teddy bears balloons and flags, after cookies. After I loved you curled in my lap, the flowing cup, rivers windhovers shore birds and I was exhausted nearly asleep: we had to begin again.

The Song About the Child

SALMAN MASALHA

It is the song about the child
Who was oppressed before he was born.

It is the song about the child
Who was pressed from the womb and robbed.

It is the song about the child
Who gleaned the sadness, and roamed.

It is the song about the child
Who was seized to the dark that came down.

It is the song about the child
Who by the sword was slashed, was slain.

It is the song about the child
Who was burned, who perished in fire.

It is the song about the child
Who swaddled in ashes, expired.

It is the song about the child
Who passed right by us, in fright.

It is the song about the child
Who quavered beside us, betrayed.

It is the song about the child
Who was embraced to our breast, who survived.

It is the song about the child
Who saves us
From ourselves,
        Lest we die.

[*Translated from Hebrew by Vivian Eden*]

Libretto

FADY JOUDAH

Whatever is seen ends
even if its ending isn't seen

I'm the one
who sits in the needle's eye

not chasm but chiasm
not holding off incoming thread
or helping one through

I too shall overcome the majority
of mourning incarcerated in herniated prisms
I too shall bury my sorrow alive
except my sorrow has bones

A terra rist a maqam of earth
a land risen I reach a cemetery
to each a cemetery
all we have on loan as tone
flickers its penultimate oxygen pair

Perhaps horses lend a grudge for the initiate
who neglects the peace
forged between beasts

perhaps a phoenix forgets
how to login our kisses
gear teeth that keep desire humming

But I found my body in life
was my heart in death
two violin strings

two strings left
the orchestra all but dead
the phoenix well sealed in a genie jar

I tossed the violin corpse in the fire
dangled one wire
from a nail on the wall its fine tuner
and made the wire's scroll a piece of bread

whose grain is sand
not even dogs would eat

I'm the one
who never was

a narcissus under the hooves of horses
now a boxthorn

and you
you be the beginning

It was already the beginning
when love was one
of beginning's traits

After Ferguson, in Culver City Studios

AFAA MICHAEL WEAVER

Walking past the trailers, I resist loneliness,
silly as it is, like pigeons chasing lions in lilacs,
or single pieces of what could be light, yellow
creeping down into this prism where we keep
what is arranged for us. Without touch, I am
having trouble believing my own artificial air,
and feel impossible, an odd mink who searches
his own sleekness to believe he is a mink,
softness under a brittle claw curled on itself.

Across the plaza I see the Creamery's sign,
a young actress wound tight walks ahead of me
to become her own shadow sliding into dark
to be a bigger shadow in the broad illusions
movies make as the lens is this: an eye made into
an eye to let us forget for a while what aches us,
the rotting faces of all our wars, hands crushing
the heads of our innocence to lay it in graves dug
in filth. Or movies make us remember and scream.

I open the door to ice cream, a white woman smiles
and offers the kiddie size to the big, hungry traveler,
and I know this is where hope lives, in cutting rooms
where the heart lets life rise from the music of our fears.

First Drink

JOHN SKOYLES

No one destroyed the day.
It died in its own good time.

Someone killed the dusk,
my parents' tilt-a-whirl

through the kitchen's
thrown-down plates

and carving knives.
Uncle Fred gave life

to night, taking me in,
pouring more than a little

gin into my Squirt,
a citrus drink

like its rival
Wink,

that sent me
to the beach's

sweaty threshold
between salt and sweet.

A second glass,
and all the parts

of speech shoved off to sea,
leaving me alone

with the infinitive
to drink.

The Last Resort

JAY PARINI

The greasy waters sidle to the shores,
where bathers lift their knees and sigh.
The rooms are mostly empty now,
with doors flung open, windows without views.
Loose shutters bang, winds off the dump.
The gulls eat garbage by the kitchen hatch,
while cats and children wait their turn.
Most screens are useless, torn to shreds,
and letting in mosquitoes, blue-winged termites,
moths that feed on socks left over
from the latest guests, some of whom died.
Who counts those sad but quiet endings?
Everyone went out feet first, they say,
was buried at the beach, where sands
blew over their pale skulls and cracking bones.
The tides washed most of them away.
A jawbone on the shingle counts for nothing
in the scrawl of dogfish, bladder-wrack, and crabs.
No one who comes here needs reminding:
this is where the world ends in the sun,
all whimpers and debris, the clatter of dry palms,
collapsing waves with their loud clapping.
This is where forgetting, with its slur and slip,
begins in earnest under oily surf.

The Unknown

LULJETA LLESHANAKU

When a child is born, we name it after an ancestor,
a continuous recycling. Not out of nostalgia:
it's our fear of the unknown.

With a suitcase full of clothes, a few icons and
    a shiny-bladed knife
immigrants brought along names of places they came from
and the places they claimed they named New Jersey,
    New Mexico, Jericho, New York and Manchester.

The same metamorphosis for the unknowns above us:
we named planets and stars after capricious, revengeful gods –
Mars, Jupiter, Saturn, Venus and Centaur,
like a shield against the cosmos.

And our common unknown we call "destiny,"
a genderless, unconjugated, unspecified name.
Its authority
hangs on one shoulder like the tunic of a Roman senator
leaving only one arm bare, free.

Names that leap out ahead like hunting hounds,
believed to clear the road
of unexpected twists of fate.

   .   .   .

And we are told, "If you want to know yourself,
	forget yourself."
But being uncharted is our biggest fear.
I have no name that precedes it.
I don't even have a place to stick a signpost
on this planet of dust and craters.

[*Translated from Albanian by Ani Gjika*]

Dancing "fancy"

OLIVER DE LA PAZ

Plate 187—Eadweard Muybridge

Small things are what call us to move—
a blush of clouds, the green edge of the illuminated

theater, the hem of a dress tugged by the left hand
as the right foot steps back so the ankle

of the left and the right form an "L"
from which the body pivots. It is the compass

which steers the heart, no surer than
a magnetic needle's shaky arm. The dancer

lifts both arms up and out so she is far into
her mind. There is no truer north. Her neck stills the head

for her eyes to watch a single point as the body
whirrs. The dress wheels its passage.

The air around her rises into a minor whirlwind
with the dust kicked up from the floorboards.

She makes a long sibilance with her dress, outstretched
between her fingers. The wind. It catches the sheer

fabric and speaks in an indistinguishable lisp.
A thick mouth which demands that everything

should be delayed. Should occur more slowly
as though it were speaking politely. The dancer

.   .   .

is folded back into that speaking wind. And
when, in the middle of her spinning, she catches

the updraft which says to her something
she cannot hear unless she slows herself, she labors

a bit to rescue time. Her head dizzy
with the promise of emancipation. With the promise

of the dress sounding in her ear with a swish.

Flight

MARK YAKICH

Jai alai is a sport involving a ball
Bouncing off a walled
Space, and everything in the galaxy
Began from history's tiniest catastrophe.

When it's time to leave
This world, try not to pretend
To feel things you don't feel. And then
Try harder to pretend to be real.

PART II

"We are the drums of our ancestors' hearts"

Sketch for Terezín

RITA DOVE

breathe in breathe out
that's the way

in   out
left   right

where did we leave from?
when do we stop leaving?

*

This far west, summer nights cool off
but stay light, blue-stung,
long after sleep lowers its merciful hammer.

*

breathe   left
breathe   right

one   two
in   out

*

There will be music and ice cream
and porcelain sinks.
Carts of bread for the looking;
choirs and gymnastics.

I get to carry the banner.

*

that's the way keep it up
in out   in out

where did we leave from
when did we stop leaving

*

I was a girl when I arrived,
carrying two pots
from my mother's kitchen.
It was October, growing crisp,
my sweater soft as cream cakes,
my braid blonder than the star
stitched across my heart.

✳

breathe   breathe
that's the way

left right left
right left right

✳

no one asks what village I'm from
though I look out from its leaf-green eyes

no one asks if I remember how the butterflies
startled, churning up lemony clouds

no one else hears the river chafing its banks
the one road singing its promises
going out

✳

when did we leave from
where did we stop leaving

✳

if I am to become a heavenly body
I would like to be a comet
a streak of spitfire consuming itself
before a child's upturned wonder

Child Survivor's Testimony

RICHARD BERENGARTEN

I'm alive because in
the middle of the shooting
my father said, Go.

He let go my hand
and pushed my back
like this and said Go,

in an ordinary way
as if he was telling me
what to do, as usual.

Go, he said. It
didn't feel special. He
didn't say Run or

Go quick, or Hurry.
But he turned his face
away to my mother.

I walked away slowly.
Nobody noticed. That's
why I'm alive.

Legacy

ANITA ENDREZZE

Across the roiling seas they came,
cleaving dark the stars and foam
with broadsword sparking bone,
blood spattering runic sky.
Kill the men. Rape the women.

Sturdy horses thundered
over Asian steppes, crushing grass,
their riders fitting arrows to bows.
Kill the men. Rape the women.

Crossing the ocean blue sailed the Holy Trinity:
Disease. Slavery. Death. The Conquistadores
fashioned necklaces of native hands,
cut off feet, impaled mother and babe on one sword,
fed Indian flesh to dogs of war.
Kill the men. Rape the women.

The railroad cars rolled, heaving with human cargo.
Kill the men. Kill the women. Kill the children.
The smoke that sent the prayers and eyes
heavenward has spread over the world now
so that all our breaths inhale lost songs.

I'm German and Jewish. I'm Native American
and Spanish. I'm Irish, Norwegian, Slovenian,
Italian. I'm Siberian, Mongolian. I am you.
We are the descendants of killers and peacemakers.
We are the drums of our ancestors' hearts,
and that ululating that frees our spirits.

Poem of Disconnected Parts

ROBERT PINSKY

At Robben Island the political prisoners studied.
They coined the motto *Each one Teach one.*

In Argentina the torturers demanded the prisoners
Address them always as *"Profesor."*

Many of my friends are moved by guilt, but I
Am a creature of shame, I am ashamed to say.

Culture the lock, culture the key. Imagination
That calls boiled sheep heads "Smileys."

The first year at Guantánamo, Abdul Rahim Dost
Incised his Pashto poems into styrofoam cups.

*"The Sangomo says in our Zulu culture we do not
Worship our ancestors: we consult them."*

Becky is abandoned in 1902 and Rose dies giving
Birth in 1924 and Sylvia falls in 1951.

Still falling still dying still abandoned in 2005
Still nothing finished among the descendants.

I support the War, says the comic, it's just the Troops
I'm against: can't stand those Young People.

Proud of the fallen, proud of her son the bomber.
Ashamed of the government. Skeptical.

.   .   .

After the Klansman was found Not Guilty one juror
Said she just couldn't vote to convict a pastor.

Who do you write for? I write for dead people:
For Emily Dickinson, for my grandfather.

*"The Ancestors say the problem with your Knees
Began in your Feet. It could move up your Back."*

But later the Americans gave Dost not only paper
And pen but books. Hemingway, Dickens.

Old Aegyptius said Whoever has called this Assembly,
For whatever reason—it is a good in itself.

O thirsty shades who regard the offering, O stained earth.
There are many fake Sangomos. This one is real.

Coloured prisoners got different meals and could wear
Long pants and underwear, Blacks got only shorts.

No he says he cannot regret the three years in prison:
Otherwise he would not have written those poems.

I have a small-town mind. Like the Greeks and Trojans.
Shame. Pride. Importance of looking bad or good.

Did he see anything like the prisoner on a leash? Yes,
In Afghanistan. In Guantánamo he was isolated.

Our enemies "disassemble" says the President.
Not that anyone at all couldn't mis-speak.

The *profesores* created nicknames for torture devices:
The Airplane. The Frog. Burping the Baby.

Not that those who behead the helpless in the name
Of God or tradition don't also write poetry.

Guilts, metaphors, traditions. Hunger strikes.
Culture the penalty. Culture the escape.

What could your children boast about you? What
Will your father say, down among the shades?

The Sangomo told Marvin, "*You are crushed by some
Weight. Only your own Ancestors can help you.*"

Horse-Fly

DIANE GLANCY

for the Cherokee ancestors

A horse-fly woke me.
It was raining and a night-long wind spoke.

The rain plodded like steady footsteps of the old ones
on the 900-mile removal to Indian Territory.

In the lightning, old campfires glared.

The horse-fly kept buzzing the room.
In his song, the night was another world.

Thunder rumbled over the past
grinding hard kernels of memory into meal.

Over the fields where they walked
their voices still filled the air.

Let the past be recognized. Know it is there.
Let their song of darkness be our history lesson.

Their world is lost.
But after mission schools and education
there is the steady buzz of forward momentum
and a song of healing for a mantle.

Lament

YANG JIAN

Take the bodies of those who died eating the leaves of elm
    trees, poplars, and willows, and place them on the altar.
Take the bodies of those who died eating cowshit, goat
    manure, and reeds, and place them on the altar.
Make them one with the calls of cranes, with the stains of
    a thousand-year-old brush.

Take the bodies of those who died kneeling on glass shards,
    shattered shells, and broken stone, and place them on
    the altar.
Take the bodies of those who died with toilets and metal
    dunce caps on their heads, and place them on the altar.
Make them one with the calls of cranes, with the stains of
    a thousand-year-old brush.

Take the necks of those who were garroted and place them
    on the altar.
Take the bodies of those who jumped into wells, and of those
    who jumped into rivers, and place them on the altar.
Make them one with the calls of cranes, with the stains of
    a thousand-year-old brush.

Take those countless, unbearable, plainspoken deaths, and
    place them on the altar.
Take those countless, unbearable, plainspoken deaths—all
    of them exactly the same—and place them on the altar.
Make them one with the calls of cranes, with the stains of
    a thousand-year-old brush.

[Translated from Chinese by Austin Woerner]

Moon Landing 1969

ALAN SHAPIRO

I don't remember now the names of anyone there,
or if I ever knew them, or even where there was,
maybe a friend's friend's apartment whose mother
if there was a mother might have been a single mom
who worked nights and wouldn't be around to hassle us.
What I remember mostly was the awful smell,
and the diffuse unease I moved in all that summer.
The lottery was coming soon; the lottery would surely
send me to the war I didn't think I'd have the guts to go to
or run from. All I wanted was to slow time down the way
a fast stream riffles over course grain almost stopping
while it rushes forward never stopping from party to party
to where what hadn't happened yet would never happen
even as it neared. The semicircle of the couch we sat in,
stupefied, facing the TV, was ripped and frayed, grayish
cotton batting under the weight of leg or arm
oozing out and then subsiding only to ooze out elsewhere
when any of us shifted, the carpet sticky, reeking of wet dog
crossed with cat piss though there was no cat or dog, the smell
unbearable until the smoke at last suppressed it,
until a cloud hung between us and the peace sign
of the antenna of the small TV whose screen carved from
     the dark
a little cave of gray blue haze through which we watched
the seas of the moon rise slowly up to meet the lunar module
just as slowly coming down.

                            Then they were out in it,
first one and then another astronaut clumsy in baggy
     white suits

leap frogging like children underwater, little puffs of silt
        exploding
in slow motion at their feet. The flag flew straight out
as if made of hammered steel, stiff in a stiff wind, never
        rippling
or wrinkling, and lit up as by a spotlight someone said
must be the earth, and someone else said if it was the earth
then that must mean that from the moon the earth was
        the moon,
the moon's moon, someone else said, and we all laughed,
not knowing why.
                Then we fell silent as the astronauts stopped
goofing around, the sugar high of that first small step that
giant leap withdrawing till they looked like clowns
forlornly standing at mock attention in the tranquil sea
that wasn't tranquil or a sea, while the President thanked
        them,
promised to bring peace and tranquility to the very earth
that seemed just then to burn in the rigid flag, in the black
        glass
of the helmets, in the very specter of our own reflections
looking at ourselves look back across two hundred thousand
miles as the doobie like a shooting star inched over
the screen and through the Ort cloud of the swirling
        planetesimals
of our desolate tranquility breathing in and out.

Death by Fire

JOSÉ ANTONIO MAZZOTTI

A line a cutting flash scars through the sky
Kalypso humans' fugitive lets down his braid
He locked the fan cooled for seven years by the breeze
Created by Divine Breath the lasting the fertilizing one
Rocks on the beach and swordfish foam
Transparent plants of bridges' armpit
Emerald eggs of legendary birds
His solitude of joyful aura cools the night

In Ogigia his drops liked to dance and he'd stick out his head
Looking for the abandoned pilgrim in the silent notebook
He wrote it but now says nothing he vanished
Kidnapped by the tides the deaf thunders
He would sing in the mornings and the ground glimmered
His laughter conducted bumblebee orchestras his thin
Lips uttered downpour speeches the people worshiped
        him and
Offered him coca and guinea pigs in his sanctuary

He loved with the calm intensity of the comet watched
Simultaneous sunsets with his Open Wound
Because the Lord's Kingdom stretches from his soles
And rose bushes grow and brush his ankles oh Apparition
May your love save my absent love May your hands
Save the pierced mountains the devastated plains
The depths where mollusks fall into the
Insatiable dump Deliver us Apu Kalypso
From loving all beings while unable to touch them

Overwhelmed by the needy you vanished into the sea
Pure you abandoned your hosts upon the crime of insolence

And now the radiant miasma the stain of fire appropriates
The shells of chemists the skin of sand
Lost in their ignorance they scrabble striking
Hearts soaked in absinthe vinegar and honey
Brightening the battlements peering into the gates
Where mothers abandon their newborns

This church slope of radioactive urine
This blade sticking out of the mast the lost air
This shriek of versed bird dispatched to devour viscera
This revolver of uncertain senses and slimy bullets
Vie before you and before you coleopterally whisper
Your healing fame of crystals and aluminum lips
Your elongated figure erecting the spirits of the valley
Your sovereign shadow waxing while the Sun sets

And you shake your orchid scent your space vest
You return to tattoo our well-intentioned oblivion
You fall into monetary manias and painstaking calculations
Powerful you speak along dry rivers through loudspeakers
You flood fears with repentance and alcohol
Apparition whether you be man / woman / allow us to
Caress the silver petals kiss the plush foam
Of mouths of flakes of eternal, returnable wisdom

Save obsidian crest of bulky dimness
His snail-like love of snaps and floating logs
His blood pumped with pollen and the sap of
Infinite pain for the absence of stars for the shadow of
Ascending rain like thorns and his rose mouth
Hail oh greatest fucker of insatiable infernos
Where the curled Bakelite child is lost in
Sleepless mass and headless lump

[Translated from Spanish by Judith Filc]

Reading About Terezín

KIRMEN URIBE

Today, reading about the concentration camp at Terezín,
I remembered the bottles in the fort at San Cristobal.

How the bodies of a hundred and more Loyalists Franco
    had killed
were found with bottles beside them, in Pamplona.

(The dictators were friends of each other,
and all victims are brothers and sisters.)

They were prisoners buried in a common grave
without a cross, without a marker; only the bottles, but
    in secret.

And in the glass vessels the names of the dead,
as if they were miniature sailing ships a child had put there.

Oh, memory is as breakable as those bottles.
We have to keep it sheltered in our hearts,

so as to go on dreaming:
Look how they're sailing off to liberty.

[Translated from Basque by Elizabeth Macklin]

The Foundation

C. K. WILLIAMS

1.
Watch me, I'm running, watch me, I'm dancing, I'm air;
the building I used to live in has been razed and I'm skipping,
hopping, two-footedly leaping across the blocks, bricks,
slabs of concrete, plaster and other unnamable junk . . .

Or nameable, really, if you look at the wreckage closely . . .
Here, for instance, this shattered I-beam is the Bible,
and this chunk of mortar? Plato, the mortar of mind,
also in pieces, in pieces in me, anyway, in my mind . . .

Aristotle and Nietzsche, Freud and Camus and Buber,
and Christ, even, that year of reading "Paradise Lost,"
when I thought, Hell, why not? but that fractured, too . . .
Kierkegaard, Hegel, and Kant, and Goffman and Marx,

all heaped in the foundation, and I've sped through so often
that now I have it by heart, can run, dance, be air,
not think of the spew of intellectual dust I scuffed up
when in my barely broken-in boots I first clumped through

the sanctums of Buddhism, Taoism, Zen, and the Areopagite,
even, whose entire text I typed out—my god, why?—
I didn't care, I just kept bumping my head on the lintels,
Einstein, the Gnostics, Kabbalah, Saint This and Saint That . . .

2.
Watch me again now, because I'm not alone in my dancing,
my being air, I'm with my poets, my Rilke, my Yeats,
we're leaping together through the debris, a jumble of wrack,
but my Keats floats across it, my Herbert and Donne,

my Kinnell, my Bishop and Blake are soaring across it,
my Frost, Baudelaire, my Dickinson, Lowell and Larkin,
and my giants, my Whitman, my Shakespeare, my Dante
and Homer; they were the steel, though scouring as I was

the savants and sages half the time I hardly knew it . . .
But Vallejo was there all along, and my Sidney and Shelley,
my Coleridge and Hopkins, there all along with their music,
which is why I can whirl through the rubble of everything else,

the philosophizing and theories, the thesis and anti- and syn-,
all I believed must be what meanings were made of,
when really it was the singing, the choiring, the cadence,
the lull of the vowels, the chromatical consonant clatter . . .

Watch me again, I haven't landed, I'm hovering here
over the fragments, the remnants, the splinters and shards;
my poets are with me, my soarers, my skimmers, my skaters,
aloft on their song in the ruins, their jubilant song of the ruins.

PART III

"No country Untouched"

Trayvon-Redux

RITA DOVE

It is difficult / to get the news from poems / yet men die miserably
every day / for lack / of what is found there. / Hear me out /
for I too am concerned / and every man / who wants to die at
peace in his bed / besides.

WILLIAM CARLOS WILLIAMS, "ASPHODEL, THAT GREENY FLOWER"

Move along, you don't belong here.
This is what you're thinking. Thinking
drives you nuts these days, all that
talk about rights and law abidance when
you can't even walk your own neighborhood
in peace and quiet, *get your black ass gone.*
You're thinking again. Then what?
Matlock's on TV and here you are,
vigilant, weary, exposed to the elements
on a wet winter's evening in Florida
when all's not right but no one sees it.
Where are they – the law, the enforcers
blind as a bunch of lazy bats can be,
holsters dangling from coat hooks above their desks
as they jaw the news between donuts?

Hey! It tastes good, shoving your voice
down a throat thinking only of sweetness.
Go on, choke on that. Did you say something?
Are you thinking again? Stop! – and
get your ass gone, your blackness,
that casual little red riding hood
I'm just on my way home attitude
as if this street was his to walk on.
Do you hear me talking to you? Boy.

How dare he smile, jiggling his goodies
in that tiny shiny bag, his black paw crinkling it,
how dare he tinkle their laughter at you.

Here's a fine basket of riddles:
If a mouth shoots off and no one's around
to hear it, who can say which came first –
push or shove, bang or whimper?
Which is news fit to write home about?

Moksha

MEENA ALEXANDER

I.
At the tail end of the year
Leaving the dry season behind

I saw leaves the color of sparrow's wings
Dissolve into the brickwork of a railway station.

A sudden turn of the head and there she stood
On a dusty platform, wool sweater

Smoldering hair, the familiar heaviness of flesh,
Aged a few years, my sister-in-law —

After all the winds of the underworld will do that to you,
By her side a suitcase

Glistening leather bound with straps.
Inside a packet of powdered rice

A morsel of coconut, three red chilis
Fodder for the household gods.

II.
Last night in dreams I watched her
In a crush of women severed from their bodies

Drifting as slit silk might
In a slow monsoon wind.

By her, in a kurta knotted at the sleeves
— Who knew that spirits could beckon through clothes —

. . .

The one they called *Nirbhaya* —
A young thing, raped by six men in a moving bus

(She fought back with fists and teeth)
Near Munirka bus station where I once stood

Twenty-three years old, just her age,
Clad in thin cotton, shivering in my sandals.

III.
Now I hear them sing
In low recitative

My sister-in-law and Nirbhaya,
That other, less than half her age,

Their song as intricate as scrimshaw
In vowels that flowered

Before all our tongues began,
Their voices

The color of the bruised
Roses of Delhi.

The Account of a Recent Travel

ESTHER BELIN

The road is in constant digestion. A continual bowel
movement in sync with my recent pattern of being
behind the wheel of a car – cataloguing each roadkill
into my database, each scrap of litter, each pocket
of whispers like the garbage trapped in the barbed
fence barriers. My travels to the reservation filter

like a giant kidney. Congressional ink flittering, like
tattered American flags, reformulates nourishment.
A recalculation like a coyote trickster inserting road
signs on my path. And I am left pattering along
like distressed platelets bouncing and bumping,
pressing and pinching along fatty fluid. My travel

is acute like the early morning songs of a Blessingway
ceremony. My travel renews as the white dawn.
My travel satisfies like beauty all around me, like
a King's longing for the sweetest water drawn from
the well of Bethlehem.

The Fisherman

Lampedusa Island, Italy

RICHARD M. BERLIN

There are heroes in the seaweed
LEONARD COHEN

Tears track his leathered face like seawater
spilled from a sinking hull, last night's catch
hauled from a wreck of scorched Eritrean
refugees who foundered in surge beyond
the Island of Rabbits, hundreds schooled
around a seven meter skiff, his right arm
winching line, twenty survivors dragged
on board before his shoulder froze
and the ship listed starboard, waves
withholding judgment as he red-lined to harbor.
They say a one armed Italian has lost his voice,
and this morning his fluent arm mimes clear air
in graceful arcs and staccato bursts, fist pounding
south, injured arm locked in a sailcloth sling,
torn tendons helpless against gravity,
nails clawing canvas too tough to grip.

TINA CHANG

1.1 Hausa Tongue

Burning, it became clear. A call, herdsman
Hours later trucks and buses. Herded. Thrust
And a wave, splashed onto every corner of world, Global
Wail, observer fear. Evil by its name. Wives of the Lord's
Resistance. Spectrum of gold, trade, thrive, trace amounts.
Bride, maid. Slaves among us.

Hoodwinked, low level, tides. Faraway, paradise. No country
Untouched.

2.2 Boko Haram

Educational gunpoint. Slim-less authority. Grueling struck.
     Poor-
Kind archetype. Woo the same man. Woo Chibok girls.
     Woo Woo.
Nothing interception, into the fray. Islamic coverings, Faith.
     Allah.
Woo. Boko Thuggery. Cement, sugar, salt. Movie industry,
     Nollywood.
Christian states, nation under Shari'a. Pimp family for
     sugar, salt.
Telecoms.

2.3 Operative Across Country VIII

Law-enforcement, commercial satellite, flying manned
    reconnaissance missions
Missing girls. Lost forever—and be.

3.1 Song of the Checkered Dress

I chortled this hausa hausa's minion, burning-
    dome of rooflight's rage, raining-roar-ravage Eagle,
      in his turning
    Of the running bride-maid gasoline air, and churning
Wives there, how she piled upon the flatbed of a truck's
    clearing
In her chastity! then on, on forth on crowing,
    As a slave's heel peels groove on a road's end: the girl
      and herding
    Tufted the big cloud. My trade in gurgling
Coin for a lion,—the dominant of, the taming of the thing!

Rouged beauty and enslaven and sell, oh, heir, thrive,
    throne, here
    Marriage! AND the flame that collapses from thee then,
    company
threading less holier, more damaged, O my children!

    No evidence of it: sheer boko makes bough down
    symphony
Glitter, and ruby-radiant tinder, ah my wren,
    Hatch, squeal themselves, and twitter chill-cacophony.

In Waiting

KWAME DAWES

for Whitney Houston

Here is a dream to have inside,
to have white folks complaining
about their lives while waiting for you
to come, to have a world of dramas,
characters coming and going, all
talking about what you look like,
what you sound like, how they hate
you, how they love you, what
you want to eat, how much you weigh,
what you are going to say—
and you somewhere knowing
that the sign of your greatness
is in how late you can be, how
long you can keep them waiting.
There is nothing sweeter than being
waited on, that is the truth,
but for some of us this will happen
but two times in our lives
if we are lucky, and three times
if we are charmed: When you
get born to a loving woman
and the room full of women
warming their hands to hold you;
or when you are the goodly bride,
always waited on if you feed them good
cause in that moment, you are all
there is; or when they roll you out
in the coffin, and folks line up

to say hello then goodbye
one more time. Now most of us
will get just about one of these,
but sweet lord, some of us
don't ever see folks waiting
on us—folks leave before we come,
folks don't even know we coming,
folks don't care—just plain
don't care. So it pay to be
a plain talking, don't give a shit
bitch sometimes, and it pay
to know when your iron
is hot, when to strike.
It pay to be that woman
who is the completion of all waiting.

Alphabets to a Home

TSERING WANGMO DHOMPA

As a guest in the waiting room of exile, I learned to build
small ambitions. I dressed in a uniform of clichéd plots
so mystery attended someone else. The future was an
    identifier,
a noun, a preposition possessing the empty shelf of self.
    I imagined
an invitation to arrive some day from those who occupied
    my present.
I would return wearing a new name. Acceptance: a text of
    fear or liberation
from the context of kaleidoscopic desires. To accept is to
    take, life.
Truth is, stories about "my people" often end in death.
    A refugee, I was told,
would not be an astronaut, would not build homes held afloat
    by carbine wings,
nor dress judges in cotton-candy robes when spelling crime.
    To get any place
I enter time tied to fate. Somewhere between photographs
    in travel magazines
and ruin of time, there is place. Like bursts of fireworks
    caught from only one
window, apparition of one of many freedoms, fire-lollipops
    that explode,
disintegrate even as we watch. We shift eyes so imperceptibly
    for the next,
and the next, without vacating hope that the lost will
    reappear. What do we know
of freedom, except as a national holiday? Weight distributes
    across the years,

the names of those I cannot yet take. I have the faith of an
    observer
whose awareness looks outward to phenomena and
    recognizes sound as sound,
so says the Lama. What do you know of freedom when you
    have only a faded
picture of home? To be free I need to be aware of the one who
    listens to sound.
To look inside, to be the center aware of awareness because
    listening to sound
is still only sound. To be free is not to be the flag waiting for
    the wind to blow
but to be water, so says the Lama. To accept that pebbles sink
    till they settle
at the bottom, to be so clear I recognize the image of self
    looking.
And the old heartaches, the winds that blow,
remember they are remembering, and find their place.

Doaa

CAROL DINE

Dreaming,
we stepped onto a trawler in the Nile.
Two teens escaped from Syria
among five hundred who'd traded in
everything they had for passage to Europe:
Sudanese, Palestinians, Libyans.

Days later in the deep,
a darkness circles us;
the unnamed ship rams our stern.

I hear moaning, splashing,
listen for the voice of my beloved.
I cry out his name.

Now I am drowning
in black water,
trying to remember
his face.

Has it been two nights?
In the dark, drifting by, flashes of orange.
I pull a vest toward me.
Near me, a man chooses to succumb;
he stops treading, goes under.

At dawn, nothing but ocean.
Others leave me pieces of themselves:
A grandfather, shivering,

kisses his granddaughter,
passes her to me.
A mother hands me her infant son
like a bundle of foam,
takes her last breath.

In the rising sun, the dead float around me
in their ghost flesh,
their eyes, red glass.

For three days, I twist in the churning sea,
in the shadows of low clouds.
I am weightless but for the babies
I carry, tucked into my vest.

They cry, I sing to them:
Sleep, sleep, for your pillow, I give you a pigeon
until our rescue somewhere near Crete,
a cargo ship sent by Eleos, goddess of mercy.

There Is No Cure for MS

ANITA ENDREZZE

Help me put on my socks. My shoes.
Help me up. Move my walker closer.
I shuffle, jerking across the floor.
O ugly me, ungraceful me.
Please please help me
out of this skin box.
No one visits. So I have a pity party
of one. I'm a broken light bulb
in a dark room.

I sit and sleep in the same chair:
It embraces me like a lover I'm bored with.
One room. One body. A soul that wants Life!
But there's only this:
I sit in my pile of bones.
I've fallen. Fractures litter my inner landscape.
I'm pulled up and fall again.

Shadows from trees dance by
in three small windows. I sit.
I've tried acupuncture, Botox, vitamins, diet.
Angioplasty, drugs, sativa, prayers.
Nothing works. My feet are coffins.

If there was a way to liberate my body
from disease, I'd dance across lily pads,
balanced between sky and water.
If I knew the abracadabra that cures,
I'd follow the sun across mountains,
laughing at the magic of walking.

I'd quicken my veins with lightning.
If if if I could be healed,
I'd sing of the shining paths
hummingbirds trace
in the fragrant air   O Joy!
and strum the spell-bound moon
with my slender fingers.

Road

INGA GAILE

I am not a boy in Gaza who awakens from a shrill whistle
    as he lies on a mattress in the school gym.
I am not.
I am not an explorer of outer space from Germany, so
    beautiful, a true Aryan; in these parts, only transvestites
    are as beautiful.
I am not.
I am not a grandfather – half-turned toward the cockpit,
    I squint, I believe what's happening is a sequence from
    a movie watched by my grandsons.
I am not.
I am not a Jewish/Palestinian teenager, rope cutting into my
    wrists, I try with my lips – the burlap tastes sweet.
I am not.
I am not an Indian woman in love with a man from a higher
    caste, stealing away from my lover's bed, spotting a
    man – he would like to be called that – in a neighboring
    window, understanding how much I don't want to die,
    the globe of the red sun in the metallic Ganges, the very
    last memory,
the last memory, what is my last memory, I want to call out to
    all who are sad so that I would not have to die,
so that I would be breath – breathed in, breathed out – in
    grandfather, man, Ganges,
so that I would be in time, so that I would be in a bracelet
    around the wrist of a child born after the coming war,
so that I would be in a moment when a grandpa buys sausage
    at a supermarket, what's new, a round metal watch falls
    out of his pocket – a moon, he of course has the aroma
    of autumn, a man, who is me, bends down to pick up the
    watch with a sun drenched hand,

a girl touches his shoulder, that's also me, we are by the sea,
     lights blink in the distance,
they are a threat to no one as yet,
half-blind kittens, we swim in a vast bowl of motherly love,
someone struggles with words to say, you know, perhaps,
     if it's so, then perhaps there could be a way, perhaps, if
     it all were to be interrupted, outshrieked, stopped if only
     for a minute and done differently, I don't mean that it
     should be started anew,
no, simply, "touched her breast," and that too am I, perhaps
     there could be a way,
although there seems to be nothing of the kind,
there is only a ship, a departing ship, through the rust-
     colored leaves, there are only vast and smooth expanses
     of water, the sun emerges, I stand on the shore and don't
     understand how I might have managed it all, in such a
     short while, in such a strange form, for I only wanted
     what's best,
a young woman is standing behind me, her belly bloated,
     and I feel sorry for her, of course.

At the foot of the bed sits an old hag with a gun, an elephant
     is on the terrace, in a lotus of Buddha,
I am squeezed between Deleuze and Body, I like it,
a baby begins to cry in the neighboring flat,
I see them awaken,
his arm thrown across her round belly, and she says:
I am not, truly, I am not.

[*Translated from Latvian by Ieva Lesinska*]

FBI Questioning During the 2009 Presidential Inauguration

JAMAAL MAY

Have you always been named Jamaal?

Yes, my name means beauty.
Yes, my name is Gemal in Egypt
and Cemal in Turkey. In Kosovo
Xhemal, and Dzemal in Bosnia.
What it means, in the language
you fear, is beauty has always lived
with the sound of *awe* at its center.

✖

How long have you lived in Detroit?

Ivy leaves have taken back
a house on the block
where the memory of me is still climbing
the slope of a leveled garage.
A yellow excavator has taken one in its mouth.
The temptation to become ash
has claimed several others.

✖

Are there any explosives in the house?

The new president's hand
presses to a bible like a branding iron,
and I want to say something
about the eruption of love poems
written by sixth grade students on my shelf.
Which list carries my name?

I don't ask. How many
Jamaals are being questioned right now?
I wonder, but don't ask.
The agents have not come
to burn the pages or cut out my tongue.
They are here to arrest the delusion
of a time when anybody had one.

✖

Have you spent much time overseas?

I tried to paint an ocean
across my bedroom wall,
but my blood reddened as soon as it hit air.

I wanted to build a house
from my name, but every letter
in every word was as thin as my arms.

It would be nice to quarantine the county,
tape off city blocks, make a fence
of my teeth, and protect every laugh
inside the borders of me, but when I reach—

the hurried unravel of sinew,
that peculiar popping sound in my ankle.
Teach me how to get my hands
into the air without the gods
knowing about it, because I hear static
sometimes, wonder if my voice is being taped—
Listen, listen; someone is writing this down.

October After Mike Brown's Death

AARON SAMUELS

And skin, by being skin, is at once damp and dry—
a sackcloth that leaks what needs leaking, holds
                    what needs holding

by being skin, by being closed and penetrable
by being firm and filled with water

                    I have watched skin

be skin, watched a firm grip throw a pebble into a bay
a glass of water tremble next to a too loud speaker

I have watched the way a container can ripple
when the air inside of it begins to break
                    watched the dance

that skin holds inside itself, that pulses
& tautens
                    & begs for exit

in autumn, when the season of sweat is a soon forgotten
tide and the skin prepares to hold itself again

I watch a black hand pluck a leaf
from the center of the wind—

and though this skin will be dust tomorrow
                    now it is a lover's

careful grasp, a damp and dry palm
welcoming what has fallen from the summer

Landays

(ANONYMOUS) AFGHAN WOMEN POETS

When sisters sit together, they always praise their brothers.
When brothers sit together, they sell their sisters to others.

You sold me to an old man, father.
May G-d destroy your home; I was your daughter.

My love is mine and I'm his from afar.
I'll go with him even if he sells me in the bazaar.

Our secret love has been discovered.
You run one way and I'll flee the other.

May G-d bring death to all village gossips
So the bravest girls will be free of their wagging lips!

[Translated from Pashto by Eliza Griswold]

Refugees from Little League

YERMIYAHU AHRON TAUB

When gazing absently out the kitchen window while washing
    dishes
or when grunting on her knees scrubbing linoleum floors or
    when driving
her son to little league practice or when watching the games
which nearly always drove her to smoke so tedious were they
    to her
and yet she always did embrace him through his brink-of-
    tears even as
she wondered why he insisted on this ordeal three times a
    week
year after year when all he really wanted was to wear dresses
    and play
with the neighbor girl's dolls, she never thought they'd end
    up here.

Rather, she always thought she'd bring them to a garret in
    the city. Like
the heroines in her favorite novels, she would drift through
    a string of
affairs ever less loving. She would work at night, after she'd
    tuck him
into bed, in those palatial office buildings scrubbing the
    marble floors
nearly invisible to the executives and their underlings. And
    she would find
sustenance in the lentil soup on the table, in the acceptance
    of her son in

the throng, in the hairy bodies that would occasionally come
     to envelop her,
in the shadow play on the sloped ceiling on nights when they
     did not.

But one day instead of little league she drove them past
     the diamond
and far further yet. At dusk they found themselves in
     a wood.
She couldn't believe that they were only a day away from
     the strip malls
and the fast food chains and the stares. And this was here:
     a vast expanse
of trees soaring out of loamy earth. She was suddenly as if
     a dog en route
to a jackpot of truffles. She fell to the ground to kiss and
     inhale its
blackness. Her son followed suit, and as suddenly, as if a
     puppy.
Only then did she consider them as exiles ingathering,
     gathering in.

And so they were at last here. It wasn't as if they'd never left,
but as if they are only now discovering their truly essential
     location.
They marveled at the foliage everywhere.
Ferns? Ivy? Weeds?   She was sure there was lavender
     nearby.
She wished she had been a more diligent botany student.
She wished she had been a better girl scout. Her son, of
     course,
would be of no use in that way. Still, she would come to
     know them.
They both would, of that she was certain. In due time.

She would learn to forage—which berries to gather, which to
    avoid.
She would learn to protect her young. She would adapt;
    again they both
would. And if the forest began to shrink, she would move,
    like the bears,
deer, and raccoons before and alongside her, back into the
    suburbs,
to forage with her newly honed olfactory skills. But this was
    not the time
for that. The time now was for satisfying the hunger that
    had overtaken
them and for creating shelter. She saw a hollow in a gnarled
    oak ahead
that would surely welcome them.

Dear reader, dear listener, there is so much more to tell about
    our pair.
Having heard that such "back to the land" tales have not
    always ended well,
you may wonder if their transformation was as complete as
    this poem
suggests. For example, did her hair, once kept in the most
    envied chignon
of the neighborhood, become scraggly? Now that she would
    no longer
forage in estate sales and thrift shops, would she be able to
    maintain her
elegance? Perhaps she reinvented herself in branches, leaves,
    and flowers
artfully woven, a kind of woodland chic, if you will.

    .   .   .

You may wonder if our son found material to create dolls
or whether he still wished to play with dolls at all.
You may wonder if our mother found partner(s) for her own
    amusement,
as was once her wont. You may wonder if she found lavender
and berries and sustenance for herself and her child.
Perhaps she stumbled upon the candy trails left in earlier
    fairy tales?
And you will surely wonder about the causes of the flight
that resulted in this most improbable of transformations.

These, dear reader, dear listener, are all good questions,
and I would certainly not wish to discourage curiosity and
    probing.
But alas their answers extend beyond the parameters of this
    poem.
Perhaps you will hear rustling in the vale beyond on your
    next hike.
Or perhaps you will simply sense their presence, unsettled,
    quicksilver
through the birches. And you must content yourself with
    that. Just that.
Do not try to speak to them; do not disturb their equilibrium
    so hard won.
Let them be. Dear reader, dear listener, let them go.

Traces of the Tibetan Year of the Rat

TSERING WOESER

Each year since, on this day of memories, it looked as if
    nothing had happened;
But *that* year, the crisis flared: he rushed out, she kept
    screaming,
And many nameless ones long hid in shadow
Threw off their lifelike masks of satisfaction.
A moment turned eternal: blotted out, they became secrets
    of state.

At dawn I stealthily push open my door.
In all I meet today, will there be any traces of the Year of the
    Rat?
I think I'll manage to see what I'm not supposed to see.

Along my way are those repairing shoes, making keys, setting
    out to mine ore or build dams:
Hardworking migrants on their daily round—
Been up for hours, like the Chinese steamed buns awaiting
    hungry prospectors.

At every intersection stand extra cops (the special ones in
    black uniforms)
Back to back, girded with shinguards, gripping shields and
    weapons;
And at countless observation posts you're surrounded by
    spies and surveillance cameras,
For to one side there are always a few men smoking and
    casting glances,
            ready to tail anyone who doesn't follow the script.

.   .   .

Two plastic mannequins propped in a shop's doorway catch
    my eye.
They're scantily clad in cheap undershirts of gaudy red and
    green,
With a cord round their necks, as if two poor souls had
    hanged themselves on the security grille.
Did the shopkeeper think anyone would make off with them?

At Dzongyab Lukhang, often I linger
To drink in such news and gossip as is still shared there in the
    mother tongue.
But today the scene makes me shut my eyes tight:
In the background, a ray of light falls precisely on the Potala
    and catches,
Jabbed into the top of it, a red flag with five stars
—The murder weapon, revealed.
That sunbeam's like the light that shines upon the *bardo*,
Except our hope's not in the life to come, but in the lives
    beyond counting that are gone.

I reach a grove of willows that was cut down and is now
    growing back,
And the long strand of prayer-flags which dipped to the water
    now flutters anew;
But this pond must be the lake as it was of old, rimmed with
    green fields,
And holding but a few coracles paddled back and forth
By young men and women arrayed in silks and jewels, so fine,
As if they'd come back from the land of the dead.
At its center stands a small temple like the words of a song . . .
Dreamlike scenes, as from a mural—but one bearing the
    marks of a knife.
Is it possible that all the wounds have been healed on
    command?

Can every imprint have been carefully rubbed smooth?
In this disquiet can we live the way we used to, as if nothing
were wrong?

Darkness falls swiftly and gives me no time to prepare for it.
A column of armored personnel carriers gets under way like
muffled thunder,
And a babel of regional Chinese accents, punctuated by
police whistles, sets me on edge.
They have the air of those who always win. Tomorrow they
will be transformed—
The older ones into seniors with *gravitas* (they have no
shame!), and the young ones into jaded tourists.
Dogs join the din, barking wildly.

Without looking, I can feel the Potala is there, a stone's
throw away.
It keeps silent in its loss, yet refuses in its silence to accept
the loss.
I remember the flames of a fire first kindled at Ngaba—
No, those were not flames but protector deities, one hundred
thirty-five of them,
And they are arising still.

I retrieve a fallen tear and place it gently in the basket on
the altar.

[*Translated from Chinese by A. E. Clark*]

PART IV

"a ghost of gunmetal drones overhead"

Poem

DAN BEACHY-QUICK

Won't practice terror, today won't
Demonstrate fear; won't heed
The war-horn's blast warning the air
Be calm, find shelter; the bomb that is
Isn't there. Let me mind the minim:
Lyric shard of blood shared in epic's
Ever-wider, ever-opening wound.
I won't close my eyes to see today
What don't exist: spent shells catch
The sun's glare, gold in the dirt
At the target range, such hollow gold bits;
The threat is just a paper silhouette.

There is so much—all of whiteness,
All of whiteness: the intimate mundane.
It remembers me for me, self
I cannot work myself, work by myself,
Keeps me lonely so I'm not alone
In the soundless glare. Those far-off
Heights fill themselves with singing.
Down here there's some water in a white bowl
And memory, concentric rings—they try
But cannot—overtake the limit they pursue.
Out to the very edge they fail
To knock the dishes over so they ring.

The parsley in the garden shades the thyme
And both grow. I think they seem to grow.
I'm reading backward the evidence, index
To table of contents, subtle page

That predicts all that already has come:
So much of whiteness, like a blizzard
With a number beneath the snow, or
Is it the cottonwood fluff blown in
From the margin that makes the child
Wheeze. She tells me she's afraid
Of the dark. "Me, too," I say. Sometimes
Dark grows so deep it turns time white.

"I know," she says. "I know. The water
In the ditch is gone, but it will come back.
We'll make boats out of sticks and drop
From the bridge those boats. It will snow
Again we'll be cold. That ant will find
Its mommy. That moth will eat up hope.
A butterfly chased my monsters away.
That crack in the dirt doesn't make me cry.
It doesn't hurt." What am I thinking?
I'm thinking it shouldn't be so hard to think.
What am I feeling? It shouldn't be so hard—
To suffer imprecisions. Iris in the light.

Memorial Haibun

MARILYN CHIN

for Attila József

Ten years ago, I was sentenced to lifelong incarceration
for counter-revolutionary activities: espionage, double-
crossing, indecent exposure, fornication, buggery, constant
hooliganism, pathological mendacity and malignant halitosis.
I responded to my accusers by saying: *My dear Sirs, how
could one man possess so many defects?* My various appeals for
pardon were rejected by the Ministry of Internal Affairs. All
my 539 letters to the Commander of the Right were returned
unopened. Then, while I was eating a meager breakfast of
gruel and raisins at the Szieszta prison for the criminally
insane, three burly fellows in white gowns busted my door
and dragged me north.

Then, one fine spring day, I woke up from a long sleep and
stepped out of my sister's house. The sun was dancing
through the jalousies and the birds were chirping a silly ditty.
The bees were trilling and the spirits were sighing. The sky
so blue it mimicked the hereafter. My sister was baking a
pungent apple pie seeped with cinnamon and ginger. I felt so
small yet buoyant under the weight of this beautiful disaster.

I took a long walk through the village and met up with my
dead love. First, I forgave her for marrying another man
during my long incarceration. We knew that the blame was
too great for two small people. We wept quietly in each
other's arms, then strolled along the Duna, remembering lost
years. When we came to our final destination, we ate our
savory truffles from the candy store and began undressing

for our last embrace. First, I folded my tattered cloak and sweater, then my knee-breeches; and my ghost in turn, laid down her velvet cape and gown, and then and then, her fragrant under-layers . . .

And we laid our naked bodies down in front of the military's new bullet train.

I have no father, no mother
No nation, no god
No lover in my cold bed
No one to bury me when I'm dead

They'll catch me, they'll hang me
The silent earth to cover me
Shards of silvery panic grass
To pierce my pure, pure heart

De-Mobbed

KWAME DAWES

If you walk out into an open field
on a deep purple storm day;
you will feel the wet cool of a breeze
galloping off the gulf coast.
If you stand here knowing
that this open field is as old
as all your memories and more,
you might be forgiven for thinking
that the world is at peace with you,
that the jagged wall of black, white,
rust and an array of island colors
with sharp arms of splintered planks
jutting into the sky—a line of
broken houses where the storm
broke on the coast, crushing
these houses into a chaotic
line of what we have lost, that
this strip of destruction is something
like art, or a levee built to hold
off the rising river, the rush
through the belly of this country.
And see over there, a man standing
in the open field with a dull lead
trumpet pressed against his face.
The soldier has forgotten most
of what horn blowers play; his ear
shot to hell by the concussion
of bombs, and where his brain held
memory, a nest of shrapnel has settled
painlessly in the thick inert sap.

Tomorrow he will leave the coast,
discarding the dog tags, the boots,
the fatigues, the belts, the beret,
the canteen, the helmet all along
the highway, until, somewhere at
the edge of Pennsylvania and its clean
numbing cold, he will be down
to the basics, a light bag of scores,
a sack for the horn, and a head
empty of everything he has seen,
heard and smelt. Now you know
they tell us we may be entertaining
angels unaware, correct?
Well, here he comes, skipping.

A Lament for Military Secretaries

JIRI DEDECEK

A dream comes to me at night
I often see strange images
Every morning I receive
Enveloped draft notices

I dream I have been assigned
And the boys at arms I command
But our time has expired
Ravens are circling above the ground

I stray in bed rows
In odour of unwashed skin
Me – cowardly and grown-up
They – wild children

I dream when the fight is over
That I don't know for sure if I fell already
I do not rest in peace
Damp uniform on my body

I lost my leg in a battle
By my own body I am repelled
I cannot move nor scream
I can only feel the pain of death

I do not rest in peace
All night long I hear whining
Military secretaries type to me.
Every morning

.   .   .

I beg the ladies please stop
The playful luring of death I implore
Do not waste the postage
On my poste restante anymore

There is nothing at all left in me
For enemies' bullets
And I fear the female clerks
They have empty eye sockets

[Translated from Czech by Olga Kovariková]

Momma Galya Armolinskaya

ILYA KAMINSKY

She sucked cigarette butts, left our pillow hot on both sides
    and yelled
        at policeman
Go home! You haven't kissed your wife since Noah was
                            a sailor!

Momma Galya Armolinskaya what would we give to ride
                      beside you in a yellow taxi,
   two windows open,
      throwing milk-bottles
   at police check-points?

The tits of policeman's girlfriend shiver
while she sighs in the line for sour-cream, Momma Galya
                      Armolinskaya
   ah,
      by the avenue's wet walls yells:
          deafness is not an illness it's a political position!

Young policemen whisper
    Galya Armolinskaya, yes, Galya Armolinskaya
whipped a police sergeant with his own patrol dog
   and there were ninety-two persons watching
      (for a baker
      insisted
on bringing his sons).

On the night like this God's got an eye on her
         but she is no pigeon.
     In the time of war
she teaches us how to open the door
    and walk, breasts first

      which is the true curriculum of schools.

Sunday Morning in a Time of War

JAY PARINI

Turned off the radio, the morning news,
rolled over in my bed.

The war was far away, I thought,
and took some comfort in that thought

when the smell of coffee drew me down
into the kitchen.

Soon enough I sat in sunshine
breakfasting outside,

where a wily barn cat
(mouse-meat in his chops)

rubbed tangled fur against my shin
and seemed to rattle more than purr.

The smell of carrion
was carried rudely by a western wind.

A red-tailed hawk
hung dizzily and high above me

on the edge of darkening clouds,
the eye of some impending storm.

A rabbit flashed behind the hedges,
diving in its hutch

as I munched powdery white doughnuts,
sipped my drink,

and somewhere in the middle distance
ants — a thousand ants —

could sense the crumb-feast
spreading at my feet.

They twitched their feelers,
and the long and narrow march began.

The Mountain

YUSEF KOMUNYAKAA

In the hard, unwavering mountain
light, black flags huddle at the foot of the mountain.

Hours are days & nights, a ragged map
of hungry faces trapped on the mountain.

But silence swears help is on its way,
formations rolling toward the mountain.

Blood of the sacred yew & stud goat
beg repose midpoint of the mountain

& prayers rise in August's predawn gruff.
Artillery halts at the foot of the mountain.

Help is on its way, but don't question
the music burning toward the mountain.

Infidels size up their easy targets, flying
skull & bone as villainy scales the mountain.

It could be a beautiful day but black flags
throng around the base of the mountain.

The red-wing kite has come to pinpoint
a medieval hour, circling the mountain.

Men & women change into garments of rebirth
lost in the double shadow of the mountain,

& a ghost of gunmetal drones overhead
& slowly turns, translating the mountain,

then stops midair, before drumming down
the black flags at the foot of the mountain.

When Every Story Begins With Wolf

TINA CHANG

They begin the long and unending war with their hind teeth.
Dungeons open with fangs and the great canopy
of a story book widens with the charge of paws on ground,
chains broken, metal clanking on bark and bramble.
Can you feel them? There, behind you, breathing at your back
as if you were the last known protagonist. You are important.

This is what the beast is saying time and time again. You are
        meat.
You are vow, solemn as a seed breaking ground, fertile
with water and promise. The wolves are telling your story
and you will listen. It is a language fashioned from solitude,
forged from berry and thorn, braille of beast, vowel of canine,
a secret cadence of doom, pricked fingertip after fingertip,

until there was no blood left, only droplets of fable falling
into a lake, until the wolf leaned into the water source and
        lapped
it up. You were once captured, caved. At night you heard a
        sound
like nails scratching from the inside a box, howls of animals
you could not name. They seemed wild to be let free. Their
        yearning
you understood. Night after night passed until you were set free.

In the open air, your body ached as it touched cold ground,
your mind a frozen ember, crystallized hunger. In the future,
you hear wolves scratching in your imagination, louder
and louder until at the end of your life you longed to be buried
with that sound: a moan, guttural growl. You listened,
your creature-mouth closed to the chorus rising within you.

PART V

"Death sails into the gilded ballroom in purple satin"

Liberation—and Return?

MILAN RICHTER

Only in a dream would you dare ask your mother
about Commandant Vasil,
who liberated her from Terezín
and from virginity.

"They gave us freedom, and I and my friend
Zdena gave them love."
She did not say "our bodies" or less plainly
"the scent of our Jewish hair."

"At the command centre in Teplice we sorted
the diamonds confiscated from the Germans.
Lesser gems went by courier to Moscow;
Vasil kept the finest for himself.

'You are the most beautiful jewel I have,'
he'd say, smiling, as he stowed them in the safe.
If I'd hidden away just one behind my blouse,
believe me, we'd be wealthy today.

For me he was a hero of Russian legends;
I found it enough to eat well,
to be sated with his embraces. By then
I had no one else left in the world.

That autumn they ordered him home,
but he never returned to wife and children.
His own chauffeur murdered him on the way.
Death liberates. I was again

free and alone," my mother tells me in this long dream.

· · ·

"When your father tracked me down a year later,
resignedly I fell into captivity,
the Babylonian bondage a new generation
will emerge from. And one day will be released
to freedom—and death."

[Translated from Slovakian by John Minahane]

Those Who Return to Him Empty

ALMOG BEHAR

The body is the monument to the living
the name is the monument to the body. And in death
the body is exchanged for a marble slab
on which the name is etched. There are those whose graves
become old, tend toward death, expire
with an erased name. Then the blank marble slab
is the final monument to the name once engraved on it.
    And when the slab falls
a monument to it will also rise: the hole held open by the
    ground.
Perhaps my father would whisper: I am the monument to
    my father, with my body.
And we continue to walk from place to place. Living
    monuments.

Apparently Pinchas Sadeh was right:
God loves those who return to him empty.

And the pleasures of the flesh are forbidden to us
until we complete the seven days, the thirty days, the year,
the life. This we swore to.
And suddenly we were happy that life is a fatal disease,
that our oath will not forever stand.

[Translated from Hebrew by Alexandra Berger-Polsky]

Leaving Limerick in the Rain:
A Letter to Ireland

RICHARD BLANCO

Dear Caroline:

This island of yours—like everything, like nothing
I had imagined: the plentiful wisdom of so much
silver rain softening rock, fallen asleep on pillows
of green hills rushing past the train's window leaving
Limerick after a few days of knowing you both, and
my life among your kin, teaching myself by teaching
them to believe a poem's image and music can be
enough to mend what we ourselves rend apart.

I've no exact reason to miss you or your city, but
through your eyes, I do. Limericks weren't invented
here (you laughed), but I saw poetry everywhere:
in the brooding walls of King John's Castle against
your grey sky, in the daring of a few rays of sunlight
each day striking the steel and glass of my hotel,
in the granite sparkle of sidewalks solid under foot
on our daily marches to *Dunnes* for bacon and pears
for lunch, also bread to court the seagulls gathered
every afternoon by the River Shannon, its tidal ebb
and flow a recurring dream (you said), reminding
me to remember and forget myself twice each day.

Why should your home be home to me? My eyes
belong to another sea, my feet to another island—
Cuba—where the rain rains differently. Yet the woman
on the train across the aisle could be my grandmother

pulling turquoise yarn out of a tote bag on the floor
like a faithful dog sitting next to her swollen ankles.
Her long needles—a soft, rhythmic whetting of steel
against steel—could be a cello in her spotted hands
that don't remember or need her anymore to make
what: socks for her granddaughter, a new turtleneck
for her faraway son, a vest for her dead husband?
Only she knows what she misses, what is, was, or will
be home to her. She knows the sorrow in each stitch,
as much as the joy pulls from every loop she pulls.

Beside her a bearded man in a cap sleeps, his brow,
thick hands tell a story resting on the broken spine
of a book facedown on his lap, parted to words
he couldn't finish—too droll or terrifying for him,
perhaps. I wonder if his eyes are green as ferns
or brown as dirt, if they are dreaming of tigers or
moonlight echoes or the timbre of his father's voice.
I wonder if he's leaving home or returning. Maybe
he's a stranger like me among strangers between
points on the earth to which these tracks are nailed.
Where I am, where I'm going, doesn't matter.

What matters is the poem in the window, a blurred
watercolor where tree is chimney, chimney is cloud,
cloud is brick, brick is puddle, puddle is rain, and rain
is me, refracted in each luscious bead. How impossible.
How terrifyingly beautiful and free to be everything
inside everything, never having to say I'm from *here*
or *there*, never remembering my childhood home
where I first played house, or the palm tree shadows
down the street where I learned to ride my bike, or
my backyard with my father chasing fireflies caught
like stars in a glass jar, or the room where I heard

my voice first say, *Richard*, my name separating me
from the world, the world suddenly fallen into
geography, histories, weather, language, wars.

I would like to die twice, Caroline, once to feel
that last breath flood my body, then come back
to tell of life not pulled apart, not dimensioned,
a seamless mass at light-speed before the dead
stop of the train at 3:05. Before the man wakes up,
closes his book, forgets his dream, or vows to live it.
Before the woman stuffs her needles into her bag,
stands up, and sighs into the ache of her feet. Before
everything inhabits itself again: brick back into brick,
tree into tree, cloud into cloud, puddle into puddle,
me into me, standing on the platform under the rain
back into rain, knowing Pavese was right: *You need
a village, if only for the pleasure of leaving it . . .*
and someday returning to you, your city, your rain.

Oratorio

MARIA NEGRONI

river talks to rock
rock to shore
and shore to itself

but we never arrive
at the concert of the world

not now or ever
more than an excuse
in a day's dalliance

an accessory motive
for stars to roar

we raise a ruckus
in every birth

we rouse death
with every death

delicately
we talk to no one
even

the orderly whiteness
in a bird's errand

eludes us

.   .   .

we don't get that rivers
never drive water
but the other way around

that in its cadenced wake
consciousness is prosody
glossing a lip

hoping for anything
we toss our insolvent
thirst to the century

words slide

   autistic rocks

     to no time

[Translated from Spanish by Michelle Gil-Montero]

Empty Garden

YANG JIAN

I am an empty garden.
I am an empty river.
I am an empty mountain.
I am an empty mother.
I am an empty father.
I am an empty blade of grass,
an empty tree.
I am an empty grave.
I flow—
I am an empty river,
but I flow.
My head, pushed down into this empty river;
my flesh, pierced by steel wire;
my heart, full of weeds.
I am the arc of an empty bridge,
the sleeve of an opera singer's empty silk dress.
My throat has been cut,
my clothing burned.
I am an empty garden,
an empty mountain,
an empty tower,
an empty temple.
My mind wandered
and when I came back to the present
my country had lain empty for half a century.
My country was Kwan-Yin, Confucius and Mencius,
and I am empty Confucius,
empty Kwan-Yin.
I have no country.
I am just an empty river,

an empty lion
pacing along the sewer.
I am nothing but an empty lotus flower,
an empty daylily,
the call of an empty bird,
an empty seed.
I am nothing but empty morning
and empty nightfall.
I am flowing
and as I flow
I fall into shame and disgrace,
watching the black form of a kneeling mother.
All I am is a patch of burnt earth,
buried earth,
forgotten earth,
earth that has been made light of,
stolen,
ridiculed.
I am an empty willow tree,
an empty pine tree,
an empty plum tree,
an empty stalk of bamboo.
I am an empty chrysanthemum flower.
I have forgotten my name,
forgotten the name of this river,
and the name of this mountain.
I have forgotten that I have a saintly mother
and a loving father.
And I have also forgotten
that I have a soul that I need to look for.
I am just a dream dreamed by the skeleton of a bird.
I am just dreaming of shoes in an empty wilderness.
It is getting dark—
It is getting dark—
In my mother's tattered dignity

I find a sacred mission;
in her ragged pain
I discover happiness.
Make me empty, make me empty,
for I will keep company with the furrows.
I am nothing but an empty morning,
empty nightfall
flowing over an iron door.

[Translated from Chinese by Austin Woerner]

People Can Tolerate Everything . . .

LULJETA LLESHANAKU

People can forget everything
theft, violence, injustice, murder . . .
But not suicide.

The one who killed himself broke the rules of the game,
ignoring the script,
everyone else's long waiting line.

His clothes weren't given away to the neighbors
and of course weren't burnt. Burning would revive in the air
the arrogant cloud of his Scottish fabric.

"He was a coward," said someone loudly.
"He was brave," said another quietly. The rest
simply memorized a new flavor of death
on their tongues and palates without swallowing
like a winetaster his drink.

Only a scrap of paper left behind,
written clearly, without secrets, no innuendos or pauses,
ending with "I die" in the reflexive form of the verb.
        A grammatical terror;
he has just robbed them of mourning, the marinating salt
that could help them bear another six months hibernation.

Some forgot to lock their gates that night and dogs rarely
        barked.
Fear pulled back, like periodontal gums
revealing necks and roots.
They were suddenly found alone,
entirely insignificant.

Among other things, he'd picked the wrong time: November
when the body turns into a paranoia of itself,
bleeding a dark coppery sweat from the same spot
(nobody owed him that either).
And this is what makes suicide a natural monument.

[Translated from Albanian by Ani Gjika]

The Dark

NICK MAKOHA

You will try to make sense of the terrain, its limits on reality,
its secondary sounds — the crickets speaking pure rhetoric.

What is the year (no matter)? Stripped of remembrance,
isn't the dark a grave, an axis by which all are measured,

the final mountain? Blessed are the dead whose bodies
are buried in the bosom of the earth. Blessed are those

who no longer taste fury, who, when brought to silence,
make dust their paper. In these hours of damp

the sky will witness bombs hollow out our city. Be vigilant,
choose your executioners well, do not talk of wills.

Bless the pavements that will become your burial grounds.
For what can we give except our bodies?

Those who were your children will make homes in doorways.
Cover your heads; our patriarchs have been ripped off walls.

It's not the dark but what it leaves behind. A servant girl on
    her knees
gives testimony that the king has been added to our day's dead.

Lose respect, lose ceremony, lose duty, lose circumstantial
evidence, lose the code—my father should not have died
    today—

lose remembering, lose absence. In the absence of the law,
truth will not be written down. Lose those who break it—

cowards who confess on scratchy radio broadcast, field
    generals
and their informers. Lose epitaphs—I have my father's eyes

and ratchet smile. Mirrors betray me. What anchors me
has drifted to the boundary. What a poor murder. He should

have died at war; close combat, an instep to the shoulder
    then a knee
to the chest. Or his crown caught in the eye of a Simba
    rebel's scope

as the world draws close. Not caught off guard in a drunken
    brawl
over his wife. This is how the loss of light should come to
    the world.

No Casualties Reported

AGI MISHOL

No one counted him,
the little donkey
in the photograph
below the headlines.

A white donkey,
his life shackled to scrap iron
and watermelons,
who surely stood still
as they strapped the saddle
of dynamite to his body,
until they patted his behind
spurring him on with a yallah itlah
to the enemy lines –

Only then
mid-road
did he notice the pale grass
sprouting between the rocks
and he strayed
from the plot
in order to munch,
belonging only to himself
in the ticking silence.

It was not written who fired:
those who feared he would turn back
or those who refused the approaching gift

But when he rose to heaven in a blaze
the donkey was promoted to the rank of
explosive messiah
and seventy-two virginal jennets
licked his wounds.

[Translated from Hebrew by Joanna Chen]

Samurai Song

ROBERT PINSKY

When I had no roof I made
Audacity my roof. When I had
No supper my eyes dined.

When I had no eyes I listened.
When I had no ears I thought.
When I had no thought I waited.

When I had no father I made
Care my father. When I had
No mother I embraced order.

When I had no friend I made
Quiet my friend. When I had no
Enemy I opposed my body.

When I had no temple I made
My voice my temple. I have
No priest, my tongue is my choir.

When I have no means fortune
Is my means. When I have
Nothing, death will be my fortune.

Need is my tactic, detachment
Is my strategy. When I had
No lover I courted my sleep.

La Valse

LLOYD SCHWARTZ

Freedom ends or starts with a funeral.

FRANK BIDART

Death sails into the gilded ballroom in purple satin as
    revealing
as it is liberating—black ostrich plumes at her hip reaching
    secretly out to
each dancer waltzing by. Long black gloves. What freedom!
    What the-
ater!—her feathers tickling the legs and rumps of the
    previously mirthless
company, stuck in their ordinary, unadventurous if not
    entirely bourgeois
histories. Suddenly, the whole room comes alive. Everyone
    feels it, that
instant exhilaration, relaxation, absence of tension and fear;
    the muscles in their
faces relocating into smiles, their breaths exhaling sighs of
    pleasure, their daily
rhythms revised. Isn't she, at this moment, a work of art?
    Lifting lives
out of the commonplace, offering all-too-rare possibilities,
    insights. Are
we grateful to have this moment of intensity, of momentary
    pleasure (grazed
by the pain of its very momentariness)? How swiftly she
    swirls by
us. How easily the dance changes color. How eagerly we flee
    these enchanting
dancers for the usual warmongers, pickpockets, and
    enchanting murderers.

Emancipation, a Remembrance

AFAA MICHAEL WEAVER

It was as hot as it could ever be
where we go after life to pay the cost
of what still hangs from a broke tree
the day we were set free to be lost.

A new world is like a bird's cry
far above the nest where the things
a bird could hope for by and by
betray him with mysterious stings.

What was behind us appeared
to our forgotten mothers far away
in visions of children disappeared
by traitors and the ocean's spray.

There in the wheel inside the wheel,
the thing God calls himself when alone,
live all the things no court's appeal
can bring back, stolen flesh to bone.

It was as hot as it could ever be
in the shade of a broke down tree,
the weight of our daring to breathe,
a sudden crime, a knife unsheathed.

One Photograph of a Rooftop

MARY J. BANG

Dawn rains bombs on the rooftop
while a legend scrolls under a series:
one escaped to Siberia, another, to
somewhere else. A silver crystal ball
reflects what it catches the way a fish-
eye lens does—both bend the edges
and flatten the foreground. How can
one plan? You have an intention,
then the right comes out of hiding
and becomes the wrong thing. The
wrong time. The worst thing. We had
hoped means "then nothing." We
admired the architecture, sat in the
courtyard and marveled at the look
of surprise attached to our faces. Two
children bounced a ball back and
forth behind a wall. We remained
committed to finishing dinner and
avoiding death. How is the present
now? As difficult? Like a murder trial
where one is asked to decide if the
defendant is guilty or only appears to
have killed someone? Would he be
guilty? It must go without saying that
there is more than one way to look at
a situation. What can you do with a
building's collection of angles? We
lived among facts. What does order
cure? If not cure, at least calms while
you look at the roof. Or at a stone

boat sinking slowly. Winter etches the glass deck. Is it always possible to find an example of what you didn't do well enough? Don't you think? Small-scale hours unobserved, cities razed. The disaster machine pauses to fix itself. You can't answer the question of if a single death matters. All those sorrows. Radio signals run through rain. An hour-glass lies on its side. A sand bed dead to the world.

Orders of the Day

RITA DOVE

After the bellowed call to rise, the cold dribble wash-up
before making our cots; after chores were dealt out
as we crumbled bread into sour cabbage, then fell

in line to be totted up, numbers matched to fates;
there was a moment – before the scramble to class,
lookouts posted below the attic hutch, no more than

a flicker, a bright, brutal remembering –
when we became ourselves again,
cowlicked and plaited, flush with pocketed apples

or tucked-away sweets. We were not
hunched in rain being counted or shivering
under rafters, trying to keep pace with

our dreams of the outside world.
We were merely children. And that
brief forgetting, that raging stupor

we tried to hold quiet in our heads
as if in a brimming goblet
until the day lurched upright, barking its orders –

was either the most blissful or shattering instant
we would live through on earth:
this hard and sullen earth

we no longer recognized but would,
sooner than later, commit our souls to
when at last our bodies crumbled

into their final resting place.

PART VI

"Speak when broken"

Take This Poem and Copy It

ALMOG BEHAR

Take this poem and copy it with your own hand onto another page. And put words coming out of your heart between the words copied by your hands. And put your eyes into the links between the words made by your hands and the gaps made by the punctuation, the gaps and the lines breaking in your life. Take this poem and copy it a thousand times and give it out to people in the main street of the city. And tell them I wrote this poem this poem I wrote this is the poem I wrote it's me who wrote it wrote it. Take this poem and put it in an envelope and send it to the woman you love and attach a short letter. And before you send it, change its title, and set forth at the end of its lines some rhymes from among your own. And sweeten the bitter and wealth the destitute and bridge the crack opening up and lighten the clumsy and enliven the dead and rhyme the truth. Many are the poems a man can take and make into his own. Of all the poems take this poem and make this poem of all poems your own, because although it has nothing to draw you into making it your own it also doesn't have the possessiveness of man saying his poem is his property and only his own and you have no right to intervene in it and to search around in it but this poem of all poems asks you to intervene in it erase and add up, it is given to you freely and for free ready to change under your hands. Take this poem and make it your poetry and sign your name under it and erase the name of your predecessor but remember him and remember that every word is poetry is born poetry and the poetry is the poetry of many, not of one. And your poem will be taken by another one, after you, and made into his own, and he will bequeath it after him to the children of poets and command them take this poem and copy it onto another page and make it in your own hand.

[*Translated from Hebrew by Dimi Reider*]

The Empty Cot

ALI COBBY ECKERMANN

a baby is born, in a pantomime
people bring clothes staring at the newborn
the bars of the cot are not discreet

when the endless crying of any child
is cut sudden, to silence, it chills us
we all know the language of loss

let us search to find the baby's cry
it was not muffled by the blanket
nor the darkness of the sky

it is confusing to search in daylight
to find that what is here is not
a theatre of honest sounds

we stare at the empty cot
it is a sculpture now
more will come to view it

painters and writers gather here
a curtain is sewn from the baby clothes
and when drawn back the artistic begins

Autobiography

JOAN HUTTON LANDIS

My father put a picture up
In vivid shades of red
My little brother looked at it —
It stunned him dead.

My mother painted posters
To advertise the Fair;
She took my sister, Jane, along,
They're both still there.

My step-mother's a sculptress
With a quarry of her own;
She works in the white marble
Of my father's bone.

My Self is such an heiress now,
What failing at the heart,
Requires the shield of Perseus
To contemplate their art?

Mother Tongue

AGI MISHOL

The neighbor who pulled me out,
who cut me away from you,
likely said: It's a girl!

I gulped you down
right away, searching
for myself
on the snowy screen
of your eyes. My father
meanwhile accompanied
a silent movie on an old piano
in a cinema.

An autumn sun was shining
in Szilagycseh.
In exchange for a goose,
a gypsy revealed I would see far
but no one understood
the prophetic ahh,
the lingering *aleph* I screamed into the room.

Later you shrivelled into a thumb
that became an eraser
atop a pencil
that I sucked on until I turned it
around and began to write
poetry
that returned to me
as mother.

[*Translated from Hebrew by Joanna Chen*]

what it was

MYRIAM MOSCONA

what it was
this old dust
that brought the mud
and these clouds
that brought
the rains
and the rains
that brought the cold
and the cold
that turned to ice
and the ice
that brought
disease
and if dust
is what it was
then these words
        shall be no more

[Translated from Ladino by Alonso Pérez de Salazar]

For My Daughter

MARK YAKICH

I should have taught you that it's easier
To forgive a malignant person than a malignant tumor.

I should have taught you to undo hate
By the minutes spent with relatives in peace and quiet,

By the blanks nobody knew were empty.
Sometimes the obvious stated with clarity

Has consequences. Speak when broken.
Ache when opened. The best one can

Say about the world is: *Author Unknown.*
And yet I try following the path of Sister Gertrude Morgan,

Picturing God nearby in order to keep me
Far away from you. If you ever feel

The need to talk to me again, I grant
You permission to write any sentence you want.

PART VII

"think of the trapped wren"

Does Grace

ALMOG BEHAR

The prayers of the fathers
In the buildings of stone
And in the public gardens of graves:
The soil was caressed until mourning
And the skies until tears.
Now the cantor will call
Now it is turn for the skies
To crack naked in open wonder:
If nature does not have a partner in the ceremony
It remains lost in confusion.
Only onto God no one bestows grace
And no one listens to his prayers:
People shout in the public squares
How lonesome they are
But how lonely is God no one can tell.
Again the prayer goes back to the page
Like the dove before becoming a metaphor:
Routine is yet to be invented
The dove still has a chance.

[Translated from Hebrew by Almog Behar]

Bamboo, the Dance

MARILYN CHIN

How free and lush the bamboo grows, the bamboo grows
    and grows
Shoots and morasses, fillies and lassies and shreds and beds
    and rows
O phloem and pistil, nodes and ovules
    The bamboo grows and grows
Her release, her joy, her oil, her toil, her moxie, her terror,
    her swirl
Dig deeper into soil, deeper into her soul, what do you find
    in my girl
Thrash of black hair and silken snare, face in the bottom
    of the world
Bound by ankles, poor deer, poor sow, O delicate hooves
    and fascicles
    Dead doe, dead doe, dead doe
Wrists together, searing red tethers, blood draining from
    her soles
    O choir, O psalm, O soaring fearsome tabernacle
The bamboo grows, the bamboo grows and grows
Through antlers and eyeholes, O sweet soul, O sweet,
    sweet soul

Thin green tails, purple entrails, the bamboo grows and grows
She flailed and wailed through flimsy veils, through bones and
    hissing marrow
Nobody to hear her, but wind and chaff, a gasp, then letting go
They loved her, then stoned her, buried her near her ancestors
    My mother, my sister, my soul

Shimmering mesh, a brocade sash, hanging on a distant oracle
Springboks dance on shallow mounds, echoes, echoes, echoes

Free as a Bird

GILLIAN CLARKE

A huge tide heaves at the sea wall,
troubled by rumour of Atlantic storm.
At dusk a sound like breath, like rain,
murmurations of starlings coming home,
light's chemistry in a bird's brain
as strong a pull as moon on the sea's swell.

And I think of the trapped wren, bewildered
in our room of glass, that couldn't tell
pane from air. A flight, a muffled thud. A fall.
I caught and held her, heart in my hand, pulse
powerful as ocean beating at the wall,
fragile as the children in their blood,

slaughtered while the whole weeping world
would free them, if it could.

Radiation

XUE DI

March liberates those plants
oppressed for so long
At the first green cluster our minds

darken and sink down. Organs
mobile, we lose our human aspect
when the beast rises up in our flesh

The sweetheart longing for spirit
cries out as cars collide. A wall darkens
and days turn warmer. The sturdy

torsos of naked lovers, as midnight rain
infiltrates piles of stones, rise
perpendicular into the perplexity of

daily life, damaged nerves
Sex binds up those screams where
mucus drips. Forgotten

words, self-abused, follow climax
till we experience the lowest pitch of
momentary darkness. Spinning!

Waking up atop the narrowest
sunbeam. Return to March.
Like the blessed in bright sunlight

As if they looked normal, only
strange and sick in mind
Originals. In this most hectic

most modernized materialist society.

[Translated from Chinese by Xue Di and Keith Waldrop]

Tjulpu

ALI COBBY ECKERMANN

life is extinct
without bird song

dream birds
arrive at dawn

message birds
tap at windows

guardian birds
circle the sky

watcher birds
sit nearby

fill my ears
with bird song

I will survive

Tjulpu – the general name for birds in the Yankunytjatjara language of central
Australia

Good Morning

KATIE FORD

You to me are the most enthralling
animal thing. I'll turn you over front to back
and back again to find it's written
on the underside of each eyelid,
your original text—no place touched before,
(and I won't touch there, either)—.
It tries to read itself to you
as you sleep; it tries.

      But you wake and forget,
you wake and think you're some history
of a history's mastered history,
your skin an encasement of a misled story.

Thinking this way, you anger my love.
Soon I'm going to get simple on you
and take you far into the birthing fields
where the ruminants of storm-cloud wool
lie down in their labor and once done
lap against the lamb so it can
breathe and start to stand.
The whole field knows it:
that the original is good.
All of the grasses lean toward it, the wind
knows how to do it, how to know it—
that no matter what
beats or burdens the first news
out of it, the lamb
will remain what it is.
Good in the good field.

Clouds

FANNY HOWE

There's a softening
To the bricks outside
And the thousand-mile storm
Is leaving where it's coming from:
From the long-ago to my abode.

I'll sit at the window
Where it's safe to say no.
I won't go out, I won't work
For a living, I'll study the clouds
Becoming snow.

Not with a spyglass
But with a wild guess
And only three words: "You never know."
Now I see others like me
Thinning into the least thing

And drifting out like the frost of dust.
Downstairs, cries of lust.
Up here, a requiem mass
And light to lead the clouds home
To the past. All of us, poor at last.

Confessions of a Ruby-throat

WANG PING

In China, xiaoxin is for caution
The heart gets smaller with each step of hesitation
Shell of xin shrunken with fear 一小心
A shriveled heart spilling blood—Xiaoxin
The blue whale's car-sized heart pumping
10 tons of blood through its 200-ton body
Yet the heart champion belongs to us
Beating 1200 per minute in our chest
A body lighter than ten dried pinto beans
Wings thundering, tail screeching with joy
As we dive for our beloved, neon feathers lighting
The air on fire—there's no other way to love
Be careful, cries the mother to her child tumbling
Forward, pulling ropes tied to his waist
Xiaoxin: to become small and smaller with each step
How does a fledgling enter the sky with a fearful heart?
How do we fly without tumbling first, head to the earth?
The monster rumbles in the lower fields, his lava
Breaths melting hesitant feet along the path
How do we live without knowing the taste of dying?
Each night, our enormous heart slows to a halt
Our being, lighter than a penny, half filled with sugar
The other half as an offering for the night's lord
Oh, how can we have regrets: to die each night
For tomorrow's feast, an orgy of flight and nectar
At the speed of light! There's no other way to live
Even if it means forever on the edge of starving to death
To dive into 1500 flowers daily, to cross the Gulf
With a day's food, to be alive breathlessly
Wings beating 200 a second, heart firing

600 a minute at rest, and doubling for a flight
There's no other way to cross
From Mexico to Alaska, our 2-gram body
Full with nectar, the rest is our heart—enormous
Thrown into the wind, into the unknown
Who's to say it's better to live like a sheep forever
Than a lion for just a day? Xiaoxin—
Courage is not an absence of fear
The secret lies in our willingness to live
Hours away from death, each night
In torpor, losing half of our being
To fall out of the sky
As we fly across seas and deserts
Uttering a cry almost too human

Songbird

TADE IPADEOLA

So the world became a field
Of birds always rising into flight,
A swarm of starlings and ravens
Restless as a run of frantic locusts. . . .

And I heard the songbird's call, sonorous
To birds of all seasons to converge
With their chorus of mellow harmonies
And their music of manifold melodies
Plural as the provenance of proverbs –

Sang the songbird: share my perch
Upon this mount of visions
Fellow me with songs beyond haruspications;
Come, share with me your own songs
And let's incline our ears to each other.

So sang the songbird to the conference,
Her luminous voice a resounding echo
Of her rich fluorescent feathers.
And I heard a chorus rising where birds rose
A moving chorus meant for birds
Of every plumage:

'The world is a wondrous egg
A wondrous egg, a wondrous egg
The world is a wondrous egg
And it sits on a nest of words.'

Words . . . mules of meaning, Atlas
That shoulders the planet, let

Me have you in my pouch, not around
My neck, when called upon to account,
Let me be found busy in your loom
With strand on strand of substance.

Words. Wild as waterfalls, you cascade
With the heat of summer in rap songs
And tonight, at a night club in Baghdad,
Only the wise will heed your cautious
Portents. Words! You roll through winter
In stadium after stadium, powering anthems
Of soccer lovers in deep play, you never
Walk alone, you lead the dance across
The fecund face of the moon. Words,
Your tenderness turns into a gardener
Of flowers on the fields of Kigali and Darfur,
Your hands free caged birds in Seoul and Pyongyang.

The songbird sang through harmattan and rain
Of the wondrous, wondrous egg,
The starlings and ravens chorused
Of the nest that holds the egg.

Their voices are a stream
Running over cool stones, singing:

'The world is a wondrous egg
A wondrous egg, a wondrous egg
The world is a wondrous egg
And it sits on a nest of words.'

Regreen

JUSTIN QUINN

Green comes even so
from cracked concrete, bare
black branches. The doe
rocks to the roe-deer.
Pollen everywhere,
on me, even here,

as I walk past the fields, along the road.

Summer's coming in,
is the track I sing.
Inside a dark inn
the girl who brings my beer
has lots of the spring
in her, oh, even here.

Then I walk towards the fields, along the road.

There are people packed
like leaves through the ground
in each plot and tract,
dozing, year on year,
tossing and turning round
gently — even here

where I walk past the fields, along the road.

These ones sing their airs
from lodgings in the earth,
asking me, who cares,

and who'd like to hear
what they've left of mirth
even now and here,

when I walk past the fields, along the road.

I will rot like wood
no matter how I flee.
Still, the day is good.
Old songs learnt by ear
make free, oh, make free
with me — even here

as I walk past the fields, along the road.

PART VIII

"towards a promised freedom"

Long Live Life!

FRANCISCO X. ALARCÓN

in xochitl in cuicatl
in ixtli in yollotl
in tonatiuh in tlanextia!

may the flower, the song,
the face reflecting the heart
shine forever as Sun!

down with walls
separating us
and oppressing us

down with fences
ruining landscapes
and horizons

down with gates
that remain locked up
under key

no more padlocks,
deadbolts, latches,
bars or chains

enough of dogmas,
taboos, prejudices
and presumptions

no more half-
truths, white lies
and falsehoods

.   .   .

hooray free fresh
mountain and sea air
without a meter

way to go birds
and borderless
butterflies

bravo dolphins
tossing themselves high
in the air out of joy

down with death!
long live life
giving out life to all!

in xochitl in cuicatl
in ixtli in yollotl
in tonatiuh in tlanextia!

may the flower, the song,
the face reflecting the heart
shine forever as Sun!

A fourteen-line poem on independent study

JULIE CARR

1. one burning lyric
2. stayed sayless
3. our technique's so feline
4. it takes its time
5. like a trail of ants
6. across a hall
7. nothing's not
8. born
9. a primate a psyche
10. an umbrage a rag
11. say God in the
12. beaten air's
13. birds we'll eventually
14. be

Hazel McCausland Lummis
at the Arc de Triomphe

SUZANNE LUMMIS

So cold, that town, that my mother's
mother baked potatoes in the a.m.
for her girl, so she could wrap her hands
around two lumps of heat, off to school,
trudging past the shocked white trees.
The air, my mother told me, where
it touched, seared the skin. And, God,
she wanted so much more than that
bare bones town could give, spot
of ground those Scottish miners
staked out the century just before,
where they worked the frozen soil, worked
and fell, were shoveled in, and their children
stayed, and their babies dropped
from them and didn't leave.
My mother grew up wanting out.
But it didn't hit her, age eighteen,
with one suitcase, one canvas bag,
as the Greyhound rolled past the address
farthest out. Nor later did it hit her,
among the mists and throated foghorns
in the city where she married, and—think
of this—became, after the men had left
for war, the third woman ever hired
in the U.S. Secret Service. "Secretaries,"
she confided in me once, low voiced,
as if the world might hear, "but, fact is,
Agnes, Doris and I, we *ran* that office."
And in those years in Palermo, on those warm,

soft sands—little painted changing cabins
all along, shadowy inside, smelling
of seaweed and sun-cracked wood—
even then it didn't quite sink in.
It took Paris. "Mommy," I said because
I was five and talked like that back then,
"what's wrong?" I know now that rising,
swelling monument was not dreamed up
for her, or for any small-town girls, but
for the glory of Napoleon and his Napoleonic
wars, his Napoleonic men—and the elegant
draped figures, the athletic nudes, hailed
a different kind of victory. But why
make fun? Isn't it, after all, beautiful?
Regardless? And, isn't it true
that sometimes it takes a small thing,
and sometimes something whopping big?
"What's wrong?" I ask my mother, because
we are standing right before it, the big arch.
"I did it," she says—and this is when I learn
tears can be happy—"I *did* it.
I got the hell out of Forsythe, Montana."

Soundtrack for Leaving Earth

ADRIAN MATEJKA

NASA's Voyager 1 spacecraft officially is the first human-made object to venture into interstellar space. The 36-year-old probe is about 12 billion miles from our sun.

NASA PRESS RELEASE, SEPTEMBER 12, 2013

After all the sonic space
& static lead in of Earthly

atmosphere, the moon
is the same shape as a record,

which is shaped the same
as the luminous afro framing

some future astronaut's face
like an arpeggio of stars

would if stars were hollowed
like the half notes ascending

from Earth's rough creeks
& broken trees—& the little

girl running through a quick
split of wobbly sunlight—

& the vanity in red birds
flocking skyward like a chorus

of singing mouths—instead
of incandescent suns halving

themselves outside of a space
probe on its ungainly way

from here to whatever waits
after the needy gravity

& humidity of this place.
They all rise like that—

round barometers, humbling
suns, black astronauts,

Mozart & his gyre of birds
& a mother bending through

the gauze to kiss her daughter
below a red & orange

arabesque of leaves—all
lathed on the gold record

spinning inside *Voyager 1*
as it finally makes its way out

of our high-styling heliosphere,
antennae blinking as sharply

as a needle in the lead out
of the recordable world.

Story

HAN DONG

The leaver keeps turning to look back
The stayer has already started cleaning up.

She throws the windows open, lets in fresh air
Turns on the music, wields the broom.

Leaps into a liberating dance with the broom
Is in a rush to put the trash outside the door.

The leaver sees the light, star-like, in the window
His life's lighthouse, his sun.

The chill light recedes, bright against the blackness
The night reveals the shapes of waves.

The stayer stays, solitary but well.
The leaver vanishes, absorbed into the night.

This story has no conclusion.

[Translated from Chinese by Nicki Harman]

Rune

RICHARD HOFFMAN

A day nears, feast
of a saint unborn,
unlike our forebears'
or any we have known.

We know how dark
are powers kept in darkness
(a broken lock, a stopped clock,
masks and lies).

When we wake
that unexampled day
will we believe ourselves
free or broken?

Sonnets from the River in Our Blood

WANG PING

XIII

For Chen Guangcheng, the Blind Lawyer from China

This is my eye—blindly—in the river wild and fast
Through the steely gaze, towards a promised freedom

Rumors storm, back and forth, between ocean currents
Machines clank to grind a small man's plea for freedom

Not for asylum or paradise, not for money or fame
All I want is a room in this giant country, a freedom

To take children to school, to guide my sisters out
Of the maze, free to be mothers again, free

To raise the young, grow old in peace, a place where
Hunger, prison or death can't blackmail freedom

Where the poor, the blind, the colored, the small
Can live in dignity and joy. Freedom is never free

Must pave with eyes, ears, hands . . . brick by brick
With a heart willing to bleed till it breaks free

The Day of Light

ERNESTO SANTANA

They make us believe that light will no longer come,
that we live in a forgotten region, outside the map,
that pain will be our only way of existing
under this unreachable simulation of light.

The sons were fathers who are now grandfathers
and the grandsons grow up in phantom cities.
To believe or to create the light — there is no other path.
There are other hands beyond our hands
holding the light or we will not have anything.

The children are wandering in their hideouts, mute,
the women susurrate, faking a state of calmness
whilst men peek from porticos
in small groups, deciphering noises and shadows
which grow darker with each instant
whilst the day of light comes closer.

Amongst the penumbra and the multitude no one has a face,
the earth firmly closes in and it does not embrace us any longer,
the sky flew away, searching or fleeing like birds
and we still keep singing the songs of our fathers,
singing low, but hoping we will reach a day of light
made with our hands.

The dream does not end after our dream,
time after time we will go as prisoners to the great Babylonia.
Time after time we will sing the songs of our fathers
next to rivers, at night,
weaving little by little, without ceasing, the day of light.

[Translated from Spanish by Pablo Pérez González]

Ama-ar-gi

DUNYA MIKHAIL

Our clay tablets are cracked
Scattered, like us, are the Sumerian letters
"Freedom" is inscribed this way:
Ama-ar-gi

This, then, is how the maps grew borders
The birds don't know it yet
they leave their droppings wherever they want
their songs, like exiles, might pass by anywhere

There are no borders in Paradise
neither spoils nor victors
there are no victors at all
Paradise is Ama-ar-gi

There are no borders in Hell
neither losses nor demons
there are no demons at all
Hell is Ama-ar-gi

Ama-ar-gi might be a moon that follows us home
a shadow that stumbles on its true self
beads from a bracelet strung or broken together
a secret the tree keeps for centuries

Maybe it's what crowds the prisoner's heart
what shines around the pebbles in the embrace of the sun
what's mixed with drops of water among the rocks
what seeps out from the dead into our dreams

Maybe it's a flower borne to you
or thrown into the air
or hanging there alone
a flower that will live and die without us

Ama-ar-gi
that's how we return to the mother
strangers from strangers
inhaling-exhaling from inhaling-exhaling

Thus, like all of you
we breathe Ama-ar-gi
and before we shed our first tears
we weep Ama-ar-gi

Ama-ar-gi is a Sumerian word that means "freedom" and "returning to the mother."

Free, Free, Free

MARY KIMANI

Pain can't touch me no more,
It can't wound me
Can't cripple me,
Can't tear me apart as it once did.

Pain can't touch me no more,
It can't take away my hopes
Can't take away my dreams,
Can't steal away my future.

Pain can't touch me like it once did,
Can't touch me deep and cruel
Can't be torn or broken
Leave me numb and
Uncomprehending,
Leave me wounded and hurting,
Pain can't touch me no more,
For I am free, I am free, I am free.

I have left behind the bonds with which pain tied me
Left behind the memories that held me captive
Pain can't hold me no more
Can't tell me when to laugh and when to cry
Pain can't hold me captive no more,
I am free, I am free, I am free.

Our city still has its forest of graves
Still has spaces left gaping by lost ones
Still echo with haunting stillness
The loss and sadness still hang heavy in the air,

But it can't hold us captive no more,
For we have rebuilt our torn places
We have nursed our hurt and wounded
We have honored the many that are gone
We have learned to live again
Re-learned how to laugh,
Learned even to love and trust again.

Death and pain can't hurt us no more
They done their worst but we have remained.
We are free, we are free, we are free.

For we have prevailed
We have overcome,
We have lived on.

Pain can't touch us no more, not like it once did,
We are free, we are free, we are free.

Acknowledgments

This poetry anthology would not have been possible without the contribution of so many gifted artists from across the globe. I thank the poets who so enthusiastically embraced this project for your generosity of spirit, your thoughtful and musical ways with language, and your astounding ability and commitment to raise our collective consciousness and make us look outside and within ourselves. From the bottom of my heart, I thank each and every one of you.

My thanks to the translators, whose sensitivity and ability to navigate the nuances, linguistic landscapes, and flavor of the texts has heightened my appreciation for what you do so beautifully.

Deep thanks to Lauren Wohl, my trusted guide through the publishing world; to Joanna Volpe at New Leaf Literary & Media and Lisa Pemstein at the Terezín Music Foundation (TMF), who were instrumental in finding the perfect home for this anthology; and to Helene Atwan at Beacon Press, who made the rigorous process of the editing and design of this anthology both an education and a joy.

Heartfelt thanks to my dear friends and generous supporters Carol and Joe Reich and Cindy and Ollie Curme, for their stalwart enthusiasm and support in this and so many other creative endeavors. And special gratitude to Dr. Anna Ornstein, Stephen Falk, and Debora Ramos at TMF and to Lynn Larsen Jr. and Ying Ding.

To Kate and Sarah, your love, support, and humor day in and day out helped fuel my passion and determination to bring this anthology to fruition.

From inception to reality, putting together this anthology has been one of the richest and most gratifying endeavors in my professional life. To all connected with this special collection, you are each reminders of the infinite beauty of human spirit and compassion.

TEREZÍN
MUSIC
FOUNDATION

Terezín Music Foundation (TMF) is a nonprofit organization dedicated to preserving the power of the creative voice to defy oppression.

We are inspired by the artists incarcerated in Terezín—composers Pavel Haas, Gideon Klein, Hans Krása, Viktor Ullmann, and others—who wrote music that testifies to the human capacity to create beauty in the midst of horror. TMF has championed their music and legacy throughout the world; in that spirit, we strive to fulfill their unrealized roles as artists and mentors.

TMF produces new commissions, concerts, recordings, commemorative events, master classes, and Holocaust education programs in the United States and Europe.

TMF Commissions, composed by emerging artists around the world, stand as a living memorial and tribute to the artists lost in the Shoah. They form a significant contribution to the chamber repertoire and are premiered by celebrated musicians in the great concert venues of the world.

> *"How fortunate that TMF is so devoted to giving voice through music to people whose voices were tragically silenced."*
>
> YO-YO MA

www.terezinmusic.org

Mark Ludwig

Mark Ludwig strives to combine his scholarship, teaching, and performance endeavors with social causes having a particular emphasis on issues of intolerance and freedom of expression. He has participated as a performing artist on numerous CDs and in performances to benefit causes in the United States and abroad in Sarajevo, Darfur, Tibet, and Roma communities in Central Europe. A Fulbright scholar of Holocaust music and director of the Terezín Music Foundation, Mr. Ludwig performs and lectures worldwide on this repertoire and its history. He is a violist in the Boston Symphony Orchestra and a founding member of the Hawthorne String Quartet. He teaches the course Music and Art in the Third Reich at Boston College.

Please visit the dedicated *Liberation* website for poet biographies, readings, events, and poems set to music commissioned by the Terezín Music Foundation at www.LiberArte.org.